easy country crafts

easy country crafts

susie lacome

illustrated by penny brown

M·Q·P

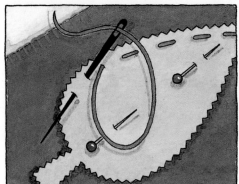

Published by MQ Publications Ltd.
254–258 Goswell Road, London EC1V 7EB

Copyright © MQ Publications Ltd, 1998
Text © MQ Publications Ltd., 1998
Designs © Susie Lacome 1998

Editors Ljiljana Baird and Simona Hill
Designer Alison Shackleton
Photographer Lucy Mason
Illustrator Penny Brown

A CIP catalogue record for this book is available from the British Library

ISBN: 1-897954-98-0

Printed and bound in Italy

1 3 5 7 9 8 6 4 2

contents

introduction

Easy Country Crafts is for those aspiring crafty people who long to make something homemade to decorate their homes or give as gifts but never quite know where to start. My book is for those who enjoy dabbling with ideas, who might not know which craft they might like to pursue with a serious interest or who have held back because of time constraints, or no opportunity to give their whole attention to a project.

I have chosen 'country style' as my theme. For many of us, this popular decorating style represents an often idealised lifestyle, reflecting wholesome images of healthy living, free from pressures and where we have sufficient time for each other and some left over to spend on ourselves. While recognising that living in the country is not a practical choice for many, we can all create a corner of it in our own homes. Our choice of accessories and furnishing are those items which make a house a home. For many of us the appeal of making something homemade is the opportunity to add a stamp of individuality to our surroundings.

With busy people in mind, I have designed an array of appealing, contemporary projects using a cross-section of exciting and simple crafts. None of these projects involve a huge amount of preparation, space or time to make.

Wherever possible, I have designed projects that can easily be made at the kitchen table, with materials that can be found in the home or bought at a local craft supplier or department store. Most of these projects can be made by a beginner – as a guide I have listed the length of time it should take to make each project, erring on the side of generosity. I have also marked those projects which a young child would have no problem in making. My book offers the opportunity to create quickly a small piece of country charm without possessing well-honed craft skills and is intended to be an inspirational guide.

I have divided the 30 projects into five chapters – Spring Awakening, Kitchen Matters, Outdoor Life, Things for a Rainy Day and Seasonal Cheer. Each chapter has been designed to incorporate a range of crafts, as well as projects that are suitable for children to make and projects that can be made quickly, picked up and put down as time allows, as well as those projects which are more complex and require more attention.

Spring Awakening incorporates seasonal colours and motifs. A palette of powder blue, pastel pink, pale green, lemon and lilac create a warm, fresh canvas for my spring table setting. Floral motifs of daffodils, tulips and primulas abound on these fabric and paper projects.

For complete beginners paper-craft offers instant projects and a versatile medium to work with. We probably all remember as children cutting up, sticking and applying paper shapes to a background. My methods here recall those childhood skills. These paper primulas, decorated gift bags and paper collage greeting cards are simple to make and look most effective when made in bold and bright textured paper. For those who enjoy sewing, the Easter tea cosy and felt egg cosies offer a creative challenge. Felt is easy to work with: it does not fray when cut so there are never any awkward edges to turn in. Added to that, all my motifs are bonded to their background using time-saving fusible web. Their shapes are decorated with simple, bold embroidery stitches and beads and buttons.

Kitchen Matters introduces some novel and contemporary projects using age-old craft skills adapted and simplified to make them practical. The painted kitchen tiles – ideal for a splash back – show you how to add decoration to your walls without the expense and inconvenience of re-tiling. The age-old craft of sgrafitto has been simplified from its original form but the principle remains the same – scratching away paint to create the impression of texture. Painting ready-attached tiles allows you to introduce and repeat colour and motifs. Similarly the punched metal foil egg larder has the look of a bygone age but with all the appeal of a modern practical accessory.

Summer comfort is the theme of the Outdoor Life chapter. My projects include an attractive picnic setting complete with cutlery roll placemat, a space for a napkin and baguette holder. For those handy with wood, the colourful bird houses are an easy project that incorporate painting and stencilling techniques. Perfect your techniques, then move on to the ambitious garden bench. For entertaining, painted glass candle holders tied to the boughs of trees like lanterns provide soft lighting.

The colours, texture and warmth of autumn provided the inspiration for the Rainy Day projects. A luxurious lap quilt with bold appliqué leaves, a new cover for an old lampshade, a needlework sewing box ingeniously crafted from a wicker cutlery container and an album cover or portfolio decorated with ivy leaves, trapped between layers of waxed paper.

My final chapter has been designed with Christmas in mind. Wreaths fashioned from twigs can be prepared at the end of the summer. When pruning your garden take the longest, healthiest twigs and coax them into a garland shape while the wood is pliable. For the tree these novel dough decorations can be made in advance and the cute angel dolls are nothing more than wooden pegs.

S P R I N G

A W A K E N I N G

easter tea cosy

This Easter tea cosy is an ideal project for those who like sewing and want to extend their appliqué skills. The felt appliqué shapes are easy to handle and will not fray, while the random arrangement of shapes allows scope to make up your own design from the patterns provided.

FINISHED SIZE 15½ X 10½IN/39.5 X 26.75CM EXCLUDING BUTTERFLY

DETAIL OF APPLIQUE ON BACK
OF TEA COSY

materials

Blue linen: 12in/30cm

Yellow polka dot cotton:

12in/30cm

2oz/50gm wadding:

12in/30cm

Selection of felt scraps in an

assortment of colours

Felt with adhesive backing

Buttons and beads for

decoration

Selection of embroidery

threads

One purple pipe cleaner

Thin cardboard and glue

Tracing paper and pencil

TEMPLATES: SEE PAGES
108–110

🕯 MADE IN A WEEKEND

cutting

1 Trace the patterns provided for the cosy shape, the butterfly decoration and the appliqué shapes. Stick the tracings to thin cardboard and cut out each shape to make a template. Make an extra template of the butterfly wings for the tab top decoration.

2 Using the cosy template, from blue, cut two pieces for the outer casing, adding a seam allowance all around. Cut the same from yellow for the lining. From wadding, cut

two pieces, adding a seam allowance to the curved edge only.

3 Using your templates, cut an assortment of appliqué shapes from various colours of felt.

4 From adhesive backed felt, for the tab to attach the butterfly decoration to the top of the cosy, cut two pieces 2in/5cm x the length of the body. Cut two sets of wings and the appliqué motifs.

appliqué

1 Arrange the appliqué shapes on the right side of the outer casing. Pin in place.

2 Cut additional shapes for the flower centres and the decoration on the appliqué butterfly motif.

3 Stitch a button to the centre of the flowers. This will hold the additional shapes in place.

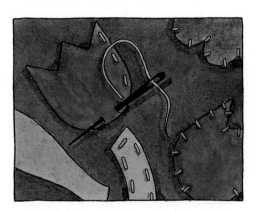

4 Using two strands of embroidery cotton, hand stitch around the raw edge of each motif as desired using running stitch, zigzag and couching.

5 Stitch the appliqué butterfly's antennae and add beads for embellishment.

butterfly tab decoration

1 Decorate the pipe cleaner by twisting a length of thread around it. Add a bead to each end for the antennae. Bend in half.

2 Sandwich the folded end of the antennae between the two tabs. Leave sufficient tab to catch into the cosy and to attach to the underside of the wings. Stitch in place.

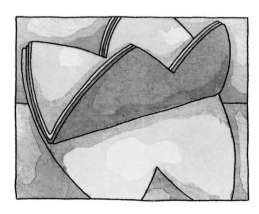

3 Bend the cardboard wings in half to define the centre line. To both sides of the cardboard stick the felt shapes. Add buttons to the appliqué decoration as desired, then stick the motifs to the wings. Add a strand of embroidery thread to hide the cardboard sandwich. Stick in place with glue.

4 Stick the tab holding the body to the underside of the wings.

assembling the cosy

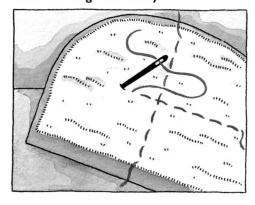

1 Baste one piece of wadding to the wrong side of each blue casing.

2 Place the blue casing right sides together, with raw edges aligned. Inside place the tab of the butterfly decoration to sit top centre. Baste in place.

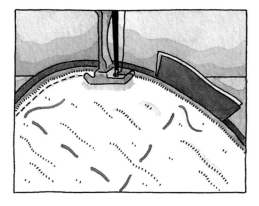

3 With a zipper or piping foot, machine stitch around the curved edge, catching in the wadding and the felt tab in the stitching. Reinforce the stitching over the tab, machining as close to the pipe cleaner as possible. Remove the basting.

4 Trim the wadding away from the seam. Overcast the raw edges of the casing. Turn right side out. Put aside.

lining

1 With right sides together stitch the yellow linings together around the curved edge only. Press the seam open. Press under ½in/1.5cm seam along the straight edges.

2 Insert the lining into the casing and pin or baste the layers together.

3 Add some holding stitches to the inside top, to secure the lining to the casing and to make the butterfly stand upright.

4 At the straight edge, fold the raw edges of the blue casing over the wadding. Baste.

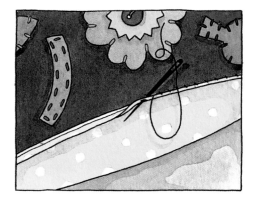

5 Slipstitch the folded edge of lining to the outer casing.

SPRING TABLE-SETTING

appliqué placemat

These simple projects made using natural fabrics are an ideal introduction to a variety of sewing, embroidery and appliqué techniques – a good opportunity to work out which skills you might like to develop.

FINISHED SIZE 13 X 19½IN/34.25 X 49.5CM

materials

Green ribbed cotton:
13 x 19½in/34.25 x 49.5cm

Yellow polka dot:
11 x 16in/28 x 40.75cm

Embroidery thread in a
variety of colours

Fabric scraps for the motifs

Fusible web: 16in/40.75cm

Tracing paper, pencil,
cardboard and glue

Fabric marker (optional)

Cotton thread to match
fabric scrpas (optional)

TEMPLATES: SEE PAGES
108–110

🕙 MADE IN AN
AFTERNOON

1 Turn in 1in/2.5cm around the raw edge of the yellow polka dot. Press.

2 Cut one piece of fusible web slightly smaller than the polka dot panel.

3 Fuse the web to the centre of the background. Position the panel over the web on the background. Fuse the two together with a hot iron.

4 Work running stitch around the folded edge of the panel.

5 Make cardboard templates from the patterns provided.

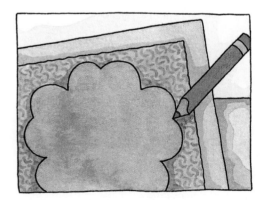

6 Iron fusible web to the wrong side of fabric scraps. Allow to cool. On the paper side of the web, draw around the flower, circle and leaf templates. Cut each out.

• If you are using lightweight fabrics for the appliqués, line them with interfacing first, so that the background colour does not show through.

7 Arrange the motifs on the background in the desired position and fuse in place.

8 Decorate the raw edges with different embroidery stitches. Add a French knot to the flower centre.

9 To finish, add blanket stitch to the side edges of the mat.

using conventional appliqué

If you enjoy hand stitching, you may prefer to add the motifs to your background using conventional appliqué.

1 Make a template of each shape using cardboard, tracing paper and glue stick.

2 Place the template right side up on the right side of the fabric. Draw around the shape using a fabric marker. This line is where the seam allowance will be finger-pressed under.

3 Cut out each shape adding a scant ¼in/0.75cm seam allowance all around for turning under.

4 Pin each shape to the background in the desired position.

5 Thread a needle with a length of sewing cotton the same colour as your motif. Knot one end.

6 Using the tip of your needle, turn under the seam allowance up to the marked line.

7 Stitch down a small section at a time using an invisible stitch.

8 Continue turning under the seam and stitching the shape down neatly, using your finger and thumb to press the seam allowance under.

napkin

FINISHED SIZE 16 X 16IN/40.75 X 40.75CM

1 Turn in a double hem around the raw edge of the green check. Press, then stitch in place.

2 Make a template of the floral motif (see page 110 for patterns).

3 Iron fusible web to the wrong side of a fabric scrap. Place the template on the paper side of the web and draw around the outline. Cut out the shape.

4 Remove the paper backing and fuse the flower in place.

5 Decorate the outer edge with your choice of embroidery stitches.

materials

Green check:
17 x 17in/43.25 x 43.25cm

Fabric scraps for the flower

Scraps of fusible web

Embroidery cotton

Tracing paper, pencil,
cardboard and glue

PATTERNS: SEE PAGES
108–110

⌚ MADE IN AN EVENING

napkin rings

1 Paint the napkin rings and allow to dry.

2 By eye, from fabric scraps, cut the required shapes. Alternatively make templates and cut as before.

3 Stick the shapes in place.

materials

Purchased napkin rings

Paint and paint brush

Fabric scraps

Fabric glue

⌚ MADE IN AN EVENING

felt egg cosies

Brighten the breakfast table with these bold and colourful egg cosies. Minimal sewing skills are required. Choose washable felt in cheerful spring colours for a practical and fun accessory.

materials

Felt in an assortment
of colours

Beads and buttons

Foam for the stem

Embroidery thread

Tracing paper, pencil, glue
stick and cardboard

TEMPLATES: SEE PAGES
110–111

⏱ MADE IN AN EVENING

1 Trace the cosy pattern provided. Make a separate tracing of your choice of motifs.

2 Stick each tracing to cardboard and cut out each shape,

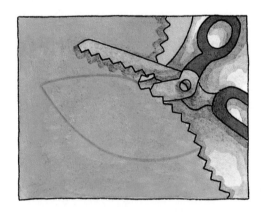

3 Draw around each flower and leaf shape on felt and cut out.

4 Cut two cosy shapes. Use pinking shears for the curved edge.

5 Arrange the motifs on one side of one cosy shape. Pin in place.

6 Using a contrasting colour embroidery thread, hand stitch each motif in place using your choice of stitches.

7 Add beads, decorative stitches and foam for the stems or body of the butterfly.

8 Place the back and front cosy shapes together with the motifs on the outside.

9 Machine stitch the two together around the curved edge only.

painted easter eggs

Seasonal decorated eggs provide instant accessories for an Easter table and an ideal way to entertain children. These painted eggs are so simple to make using paper collage and fabric trims.

materials

Polystyrene eggs

A selection of waterproof paints and paint brush

Fabric, ribbon and ric-rac braid scraps

PVA glue

Adhesive paper

Glass-headed pins

Cardboard, pencil and tracing paper

TEMPLATES: SEE PAGES 110–111

⌚ MADE IN A WEEKEND

☺ SUITABLE FOR A CHILD TO MAKE

1 Paint the eggs using a selection of suitable spring colours. Allow to dry. Add a second coat if necessary.

3 Arrange the motifs as desired on the egg. Add paper collages and any other fabric decorations as you choose.

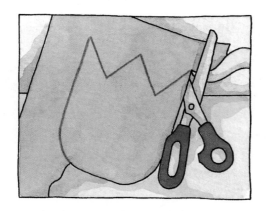

2 Cut fabric flowers and stems by eye or by first making patterns from some of the templates provided.

4 Wrap ribbon around the egg to finish. Tie in a bow at the top and secure with a glass-headed pin.

SPRING TABLE CENTREPIECE

trug

Minimal painting and stencilling techniques are all it takes to revamp a garden trug into an attractive spring table centrepiece.

materials

Small trug

Green, pink and blue

emulsion paint

Paint brush

Tracing paper and pencil

Matt varnish

TEMPLATES: SEE PAGE 112

◔ MADE IN AN EVENING

1 Paint the handle of the trug with blue paint. Allow to dry, then paint the rim of the trug pink. Trace the tulip and leaf patterns provided.

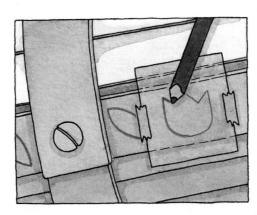

2 Transfer the tracing to the rim and handle, ensuring the motifs are evenly spaced.

3 Carefully paint in the outline of the motif using a fine paint brush, then fill in the centre. Work with one colour at a time and allow each to dry thoroughly before adding another colour.

4 Apply varnish to the painted areas to preserve the life of the decoration.

5 Fill with your choice of spring flowers, or paper primula posies.

Preparing wood before adding the stencil decoration

1 Remove any old flaking varnish or paint from the surface of the wood.

2 Make any repairs at this stage

3 Sand down any rough edges.

4 Wash the surface of the wood with a soap and water solution. Allow to dry.

paper primula posies

Quick and simple papercraft is combined with florist's wire and an assortment of beads to produce these stylish floral accessories suitable for a spring table.

materials

A selection of textured crepe papers: pink, yellow and green

Beads

Fine florist's or cake decorator's wire

PVA glue

Tracing paper, pencil and thin cardboard

Embroidery thread

TEMPLATES: SEE PAGE 112

🕑 MADE IN AN EVENING

1 Trace the patterns provided. Stick the tracings to thin cardboard and cut out.

2 Using the templates, cut the required number of flower heads, centres and leaves. For each flower you will need two leaves.

3 Place one flower centre on each flower. Push the end of a 6in/15cm length of wire through the flower and centre.

4 Push one bead onto the end of the wire and tilt the end of the wire to stop the bead

rolling off. Secure all the layers together with a dab of glue.

5 Cut ⅙in/0.5cm wide strips of green crepe paper to secure the leaves to the wire stem. Dab glue onto the strips.

6 Wrap the base end of each leaf around the stem, below the flower head. Stick in place using the strips of paper.

7 To make a posy, you will need five stems. Tie together with a length of thread.

gift bags

Paper provides a versatile and economical craft medium and these gift bags offer the chance to make a unique gift wrapping and to experiment with different and unusual textured, crepe and handmade papers.

1 Make templates from the patterns provided for the bag, tulips and primulas.

2 Cut each from textured paper.

3 To make the bag, transfer all the foldlines to the pattern with a very light pencil.

4 To define the bag shape, fold down the bag top, then on each broken pencil line crease the paper between your finger and thumb.

5 For the handles cut two lengths of foam, each 10in/25cm.

6 Clip the folded bag top with a V at the marked points, large enough to thread the foam handle through.

7 Stick each end of the foam in place inside the bag between the crepe paper layers using glue or tape.

8 Fold in the sides. Stick the flap in place with a small dab of glue. Wipe away any excess immediately. Use a peg to hold the pieces together. Allow to dry.

9 Fold in the flap marked 1. Then fold in the base pieces. Stick pieces 4 and 5 to the inside side edges of the bag. Place a weight inside the bag, such as a pack of playing cards to ensure that all the edges are firmly stuck together. Allow to dry.

10 To the front of the bag, stick your choice of floral motifs.

materials

A selection of textured crepe papers

PVA glue and adhesive tape

Tracing paper, pencil and thin cardboard

Foam for the handles

TEMPLATES: SEE PAGE 111

⏱ MADE IN AN EVENING

paper cards, envelopes and gift tags

These colourful co-ordinating cards, gift tags and envelopes are an ideal project for children to make for their friends or to use to personalise and individualise presents.

materials

Blank greeting cards and gift tags

A selection of papers in bright colours

Pencil, tracing paper and thin cardboard

Fabric scraps

PVA glue

TEMPLATES: SEE PAGE 112

🕯 MADE IN AN EVENING

☺ SUITABLE FOR A CHILD TO MAKE

1 Trace the patterns provided to make templates. Stick the tracings to thin cardboard and cut out each shape.

2 From a selection of papers and fabric scraps, cut out the required number of fish, making two-toned bodies as desired.

3 Arrange the shapes on your choice of gift tags, envelopes and greeting cards. Stick in place with PVA glue.

KITCHEN MATTERS

herb sachet

Store a harvest of dried herbs in these Provencale-style herb bags. The appliqué decoration is easy to do and the bags make a simple and attractive accessory for the kitchen area.

FINISHED SIZE 6½ X 10½IN/16.5 X 26.75CM

appliqué background

1 Cut one piece of linen 3¾ x 4¼in/ 9.5 x 10.75cm.

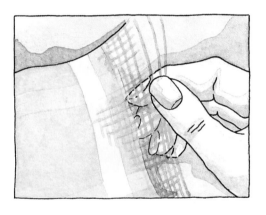

2 Carefully fray ½in/1.5cm all around the raw edges of the linen.

3 Bond a scrap of fusible web to the wrong side of the leaf fabric.

4 By eye, or using the pattern provided, cut the required number of leaves. Remove the paper backing from each.

5 Arrange the leaves on the background. When you are happy with the arrangement fuse each in place.

6 Couch embroidery thread onto the leaves for veins and a stem.

7 Cut one piece of fusible web, 2¾ x 3¼in/ 7 x 8.25cm. Centre the web on the wrong side of the linen and fuse the two together avoiding the frayed edges. Machine stitch around the edge of the panel to secure it in position.

materials

Gingham for the bag and tie: 7 x 22in/18 x 56cm

Solid yellow for lining: 7 x 22in/18 x 56cm

Linen and cotton scraps for the appliqué decoration

Scraps of fusible web

Embroidery threads

Cardboard, glue tracing paper and pencil

TEMPLATES: SEE PAGE 113

⏱ MADE IN A DAY

making the bag

1 Cut two pieces of gingham 7 x 11in/
18 x 28cm. Cut the same for the lining.

2 Place the appliqué decoration on the right
side of one piece of gingham, 4½in/11.5cm
from the top edge and centred widthways.
Fuse in place, then stitch to secure without
catching in the frayed edges.

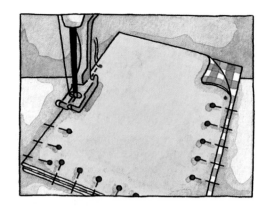

3 With right sides together, stitch one
gingham piece to a yellow lining around
three sides only and leaving the bag bottom
free. Use a ¼in/0.75cm seam. Clip the
corners off for a neat finish. Turn right side
out and press.

4 Place the two pieces, gingham sides
together. Pin. Stitch the two halves of the bag
together, beginning and ending 2½in/6.5cm
from the top edge. Turn right side out. Press.
Topstitch the bag top opening.

5 To make the tie, cut one piece 2 x 26in/
5 x 66cm. Fold the tie in half lengthways.
Press. Open out the fold. Turn the raw edges
of the length in to the centre fold. Press.
Refold on the centre line. Stitch the tie, leave
the short edges unstitched.

6 Find the centre of the length and stitch to
one side seam of the sachet, just below the
opening. Knot the raw edges to finish.

herb bags

Traditional embroidery cutwork is made easy, using time saving fusible web. Simply bond a layer of web to the wrong side of your fabric choice and cut away your choice of motif. Fray the edges of the fabric and add folk art-style freehand embroidery embellishment.

FINISHED SIZE: 5¾ X 8IN/14.5 X 20.25CM

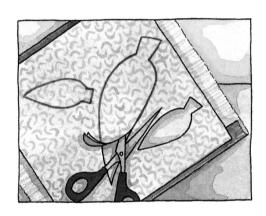

cut work

1 For the cut work panel, cut one blue square 5in/12.75cm. At two opposite sides, turn in ¼in/0.75cm and press. At the top and bottom, fray the raw edges.

2 Cut two squares of fusible web 4 x 4½in/ 10 x 11.5cm. Centre one piece of web on the wrong side of the panel avoiding the frayed edges and fuse in place.

3 Make a cardboard template of three different leaf shapes. Arrange the templates

on the paper side of the fusible web. When you are happy with the arrangement, draw around the shapes. Carefully cut out the leaves without breaching the drawn line.

4 From green, cut one square 4 x 4½in/10 x 11.5cm. Place the green right side down behind the blue panel to cover the cut out shapes. Fuse the two together following the manufacturer's instructions.

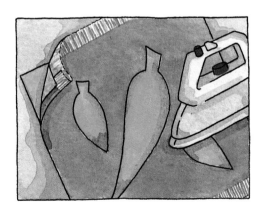

5 Bond the second piece of fusible web to the wrong side of the green.

materials

• MATERIALS GIVEN ARE FOR THE YELLOW TICKING BAG

Yellow ticking or linen for the bag: 10 x 14in/25 x 36cm

A selection of fabric scraps in co-ordinating colours for the handles and embellishment: blue, green, and check

Scraps of fusible web

A selection of embroidery thread

TEMPLATES: SEE PAGE 113

🕐 MADE IN A DAY

making the bag

1 For the bag front and back, cut two pieces 6¼ x 9½in/16 x 24.25cm.

2 Turn in ¼in/0.75cm at the top raw edge on both pieces. Press. Turn in another 1in/2.5cm. Press. Open out the folds.

3 Centre the appliqué panel across the width of the bag front, 1¼in/3.25cm from the folded edge. Fuse together.

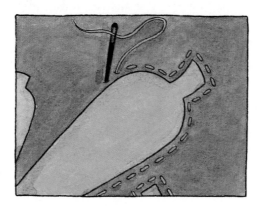

4 Add embroidery decoration to the panel.

5 For the corner decoration, cut one square 2½in/6.5cm. Cut the square in half across one diagonal to yield two triangles. Place one triangle at each bottom corner on the bag front. Baste then stitch in place.

6 Place the bag front and back right sides together. Stitch two sides and the bottom. Turn in the first fold at the top of the bag.

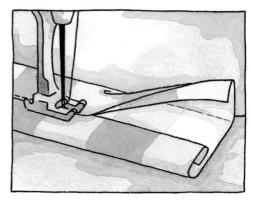

7 For the handles, cut two pieces of check 9½ x 2½in/24.25 x 6.5cm. Turn in ¼in/0.75cm seam along each long edge. Press. Turn each folded edge in again so that the two just overlap at the centre. Stitch the overlap.

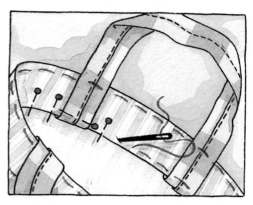

8 Position the short raw edges of each handle in the second fold at the top of the bag, and with raw edges pointing towards the bottom of the bag.

9 Refold on the second foldline. Fold the handles up into the correct position and pin. Topstitch close to the folded edge and the top edge of the bag. Turn right side out.

stencilled enamelware

Personalise enamel picnic plates with simple-style hand-painted vegetables applied using stencilling techniques. Adapt each motif to make unique and modern platters to decorate your picnic table.

1 Wash the plates in warm soapy water, rinse well and allow to dry.

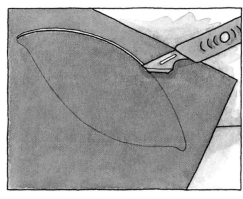

2 Trace the vegetables from the templates provided. Stick each tracing to the centre of individual pieces of cardboard and carefully cut each out.

materials

Four white enamel tin plates

Cardboard

Glue

Tracing paper

Craft knife

Masking tape

Waterproof paints in your choice of colours

Small containers for paint

Stencil brush

Small watercolour paint brush

Pencil with eraser end

1in/2.5cm paint brush

Matt varnish

TEMPLATES: SEE PAGE 114

TEMPLATES: SEE PAGE 114

♀ MADE IN AN EVENING

3 Place the stencil on the enamel plate in the required position and secure firmly in place with masking tape.

4 Pour a small quantity of each colour into individual containers (a saucer or jam jar lid are ideal).

5 Using your stencil brush, take up the smallest amount of paint with the tip of the brush and lightly dab the area to be covered. Build up colour gradually until you achieve the required density. Work with one colour at a time and allow it to dry thoroughly before applying the next colour.

6 For the peas and corn niblets, use the eraser at the end of your pencil. Dip the eraser in paint, then press lightly on the plate. Practise a few times on a piece of paper first to get the shape and density of colour that you want.

7 Allow the plate to dry thoroughly then seal with a coat of matt varnish.

papier mâché bowls

These fun-to-make papier mâché bowls offer a practical storage solution and provide an attractive feature in any kitchen. Bright colours and eye-catching motifs will add cheer to any functional object.

1 Lightly coat the interior of a bowl with Vaseline. Tear up newspaper into strips.

2 Using a diluted mix of PVA glue and water, stick the newspaper to the interior of the bowl, smoothing out the paper as you go to remove any air bubbles. Keep applying the newspaper strips until you have built up at least 50 layers.

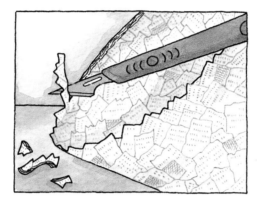

3 Allow the papier mâché to dry completely in a warm airing cupboard then carefully slide it out of the mould. You may need to use a scalpel to remove any paper that has dried over the rim of your mould.

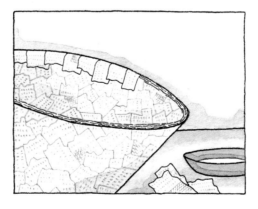

4 Seal the rim of the papier mâché bowl with strips of paper so that no rough edges are visible.

materials

Selection of ceramic bowls to use as moulds

Petroleum jelly (Vaseline)

Newspaper

Tissue paper

Coloured art paper

PVA glue

Masking tape

Empty round box (Camembert cheese box is ideal)

Craft knife

White emulsion paint

Waterproof paint

Double-sided adhesive tape

Pencil with eraser end

Matt varnish

Small paint brush

TEMPLATES: SEE PAGE 114

🕑 MADE IN A WEEKEND

5 Tape the cardboard box lid to the bottom of the bowl to form the base. Allow to dry.

6 Using white emulsion, paint the inside and outside of the bowl.

7 Using diluted glue, stick torn pieces of tissue to the inside and outside of the bowl. Build up the layers.

8 Cut the pea pod and carrot shapes from coloured art paper. Stick in place. Paint on the spots with the eraser end of a pencil using waterproof paint.

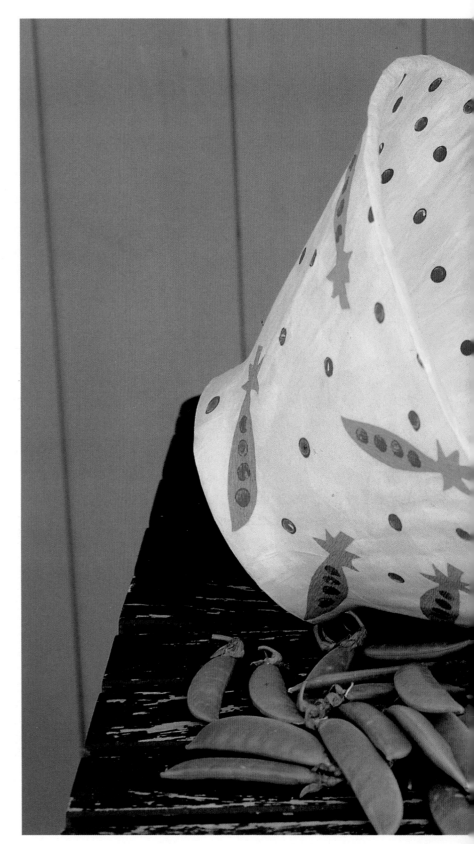

foil decorated egg larder

Punching into tinware is deceptively easy. The softness of the tin allows shapes to be punched into the surface using a hammer and blunt nail, creating an embossed effect on the surface.

materials

A piece of tin

Tin snippers or sharp scissors

MDF egg larder blank

Paint and paint brush

Pencil and tracing paper

Hammer and blunt nail

Screwdriver

PVA glue or small tacks

Adhesive tape

TEMPLATE: SEE PAGE 115

⏲ MADE IN AN EVENING

1 Unscrew the door of the larder and remove the mesh front. Paint the door and larder as desired and allow to dry.

2 Cut the tin to the same dimensions as the discarded mesh. It should fit snugly into the door frame. Trace the pattern provided. Place the tracing on the right side of the tin. Hold it in place with a small amount of tape.

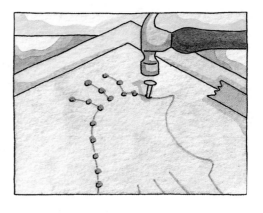

3 Place the blunt end of the nail on the drawn line. Gently tap the nail with the hammer to create an indentation in the surface of the tin. Work around the transferred shape, making indentations at even intervals.

4 Glue or use small tacks to secure the tin decoration to the inside door frame.

painted kitchen tiles

Painting your own wall tiles offers the chance to add colour and character to your kitchen decor without the expense and upheaval of re-tiling. The techniques are simple and effective – a layer of paint is added to the tile surface and scraped away to add texture.

1 Trace the pattern provided. Stick the tracing to thin cardboard and cut out.

2 Draw the shape on the tile.

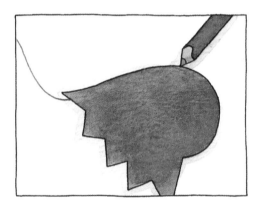

3 Colour in the chicken, allowing the brush strokes to show. Allow to dry.

4 For the border of both the plain and the chicken tiles, paint a yellow spot in each corner. Paint a blue border line freehand.

5 Using a sharp instrument, on each chicken carefully scrape away feather patterns on the tail, neck and wing. Scratch a fine line just inside the outline of the body and crown. Scratch in the legs, claws and any other detail you wish to define.

6 On the border, scratch a line along the centre of the blue lines. Scratch a star into each yellow corner dot.

7 Fix the paints by baking the tiles in the oven. Follow the manufacturer's instructions.

materials

Waterproof paint in your choice of colours

Paint brush

Tracing paper, cardboard and pencil

Kitchen tiles

Sharp instrument such as a scalpel or darning needle

TEMPLATE: SEE PAGE 115

⏱ MADE IN A DAY

bird on a twig cushion

Designed to co-ordinate with the sgrafitto kitchen tiles and egg larder, this appliqué cushion has a folk art appeal appropriate for its kitchen setting.

FINISHED SIZE 16½ X 16½IN/42 X 42CM

materials

Turquoise cotton for the background: ½yd/0.5m

Rust felt for the bird: 12in/30cm square

Scraps of felt in a variety of colours for borders and bird

Fusible web: ½yd/0.5m

Pencil, tracing paper, glue stick and cardboard

Hand embroidery thread

Fabric marker and ruler

3 buttons: 1in/2.5cm diameter

Cushion pad: 16in/40.75cm

TEMPLATES: SEE PAGE 126

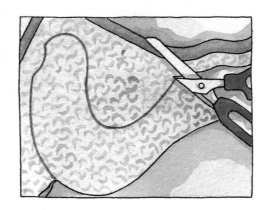

⏱ MADE IN A WEEKEND

1 To make templates, trace the patterns provided. Stick the tracings to thin cardboard and cut each out.

2 Draw around each template on the paper side of fusible web. Cut out each shape, at least ½in/1.5cm larger all around than the drawn outline. Cut four stars, circles and squares for the corners.

3 Following the manufacturer's instructions, bond each web shape to the wrong side of appropriate coloured felt. Allow to cool. Cut out each shape accurately on the drawn line.

4 Remove the paper backing from each circle and fuse it to the centre of the four-point star. Fuse the star to the centre of the square. Set aside.

8 Arrange the borders along the guidelines so that no background is visible. When you are happy with the arrangement fuse each rectangle in place.

5 To make the pieced borders, cut rectangles of scraps 1½in/4cm wide and in varying lengths and colours, sufficient to make four borders, each 10½ x 1½in/25.5 x 4cm.

6 From turquoise, for the cushion front, cut one piece 17½in/44.5cm square. Cut the same for the cushion back. For the envelope flap, cut one piece 17½ x 6½in/44.5 x 16.5cm.

7 On the right side of the cushion front, draw a guideline for placing the multi-coloured appliqué borders, ½in/1.5cm from the raw edges.

9 Position each corner so that the raw edges touch the guideline and overlap the borders. Remove the paper backing and fuse in place.

10 Centre the body and legs on the cushion front. Place the twig just underneath the claws. Remove the bird and legs and fuse the twig in place. Replace the bird and legs, then the back and beak and fuse each in place in turn. Add an eye.

11 Using appropriate coloured thread, machine satin stitch around the raw edges of each shape in the border, corners and on the bird. Define the tail feathers.

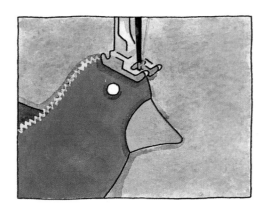

12 Stab stitch around the bird and back outlines. Make a French knot for the pupil.

making the cushion

1 On the cushion back and the envelope flap, on one long edge, turn in a double 1in/2.5cm hem. Press, then topstitch in place.

2 Measure and mark the position of three buttonholes on the cushion back – one in the centre of the double hem and the other two 4in/10cm from the raw edges. Machine stitch each buttonhole, 1in/2.5cm long.

3 Place the cushion back right side down on a flat surface. Place the envelope flap on top, at the buttonhole end of the cushion back.

4 Shuffle the envelope flap, so that the two pieces of the cushion flap measure 17½in/44.5cm long. Pin the overlap.

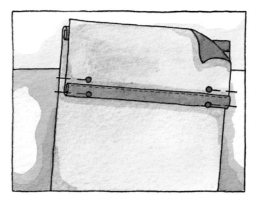

5 Stitch the overlap only within the ½in/1.5cm seam.

6 Place the cushion front and back right sides together.

7 Machine stitch all around the raw edges. Clip the corners. Turn right side out and ease out the corners. Press.

8 To finish, mark the position of the buttons and stitch each in place to correspond with a buttonhole.

9 Insert the cushion pad.

OUTDOOR LIFE

bird houses

Stylish and simple, these colourful bird houses have a contemporary appeal that will make an attractive addition to any garden. Individualise each house with stylised bird motifs, painted using stencils.

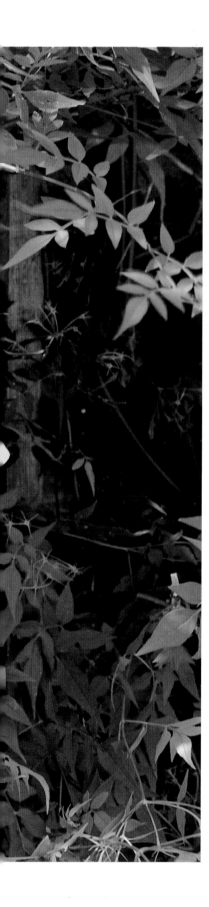

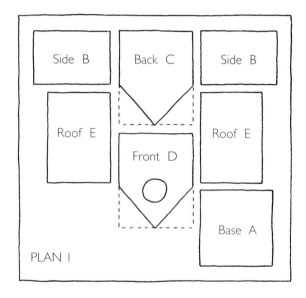

Side B   Back C   Side B

Roof E   Roof E

Front D

Base A

PLAN I

Base = 4½ × 4½in/11.5 × 11.5cm
Sides = 2¾ × 4in/7 × 10cm (Cut two)
House back and front = 5¼ × 4½in/13.5 × 11.5cm
(Cut two)
Roof = 5½ × 4⅞in/14 × 12.5cm (Cut two)

materials

(TO MAKE ONE HOUSE)

MDF: 24in/60cm square

Jigsaw or fretsaw

Sandpaper

Wood glue

Wooden dowel ¼in/0.75cm diameter: 4in/10cm

1in/2.5cm square dowel for the chimney: 2in/5cm long

Wood primer

White emulsion paint

Selection of Pelican Plaka waterproof paints

Matt varnish

Cardboard or stencil plastic

Craft knife and ruler

Small paint brushes

Stencil brushes

Pencil

Small screw to hang house

TEMPLATES: SEE PAGE 116

⏱ MADE IN A WEEKEND

1 Following plan 1, on your sheet of MDF, mark in pencil, then cut the base, sides, front and back and roof panels.

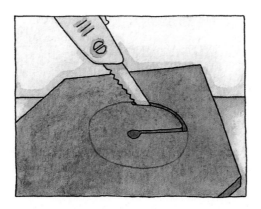

2 On the house front mark a 1¼in/3cm diameter circle, 1¼in/3.25cm down from the apex and cut out using a jigsaw or fretsaw.

3. Using a medium grade sandpaper, rub all the edges smooth ready for assembling the

bird house. Using a finer paper, sand any surface that will be painted.

4 On the 1in/2.5cm square dowel, measure 1¾in/4cm from the end on the right-hand side and ⅝in/1.75cm on the left-hand side.

5 Draw a diagonal joining the two points and cut out the chimney shape.

6 Study plan 2 and assemble the house in alphabetical order beginning at the base.

7 Apply a small amount of glue to each edge, then attach one side of the house to the base. Allow to dry thoroughly.

8 Paint the house with your choice of colours, allowing each to dry thoroughly before applying the next shade.

9 Trace the bird pattern provided. Stick the tracing to the middle of a rectangle of cardboard. Using a craft knife, carefully cut out the bird shape. Make a separate stencil for the wing.

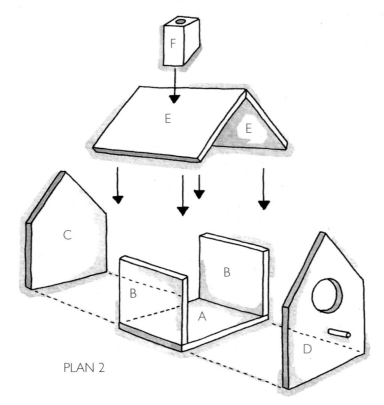

PLAN 2

10 Position the stencil and paint in the bird body. Allow to dry before adding the wing.

PICNIC PLACEMAT SET

placemat

This stylish and practical picnic placemat set provides an ideal solution to store cutlery and hold a napkin – an easy way to make each person responsible for their own!

FINISHED SIZE 15½ X 10¾IN/39.5 X 27.25CM

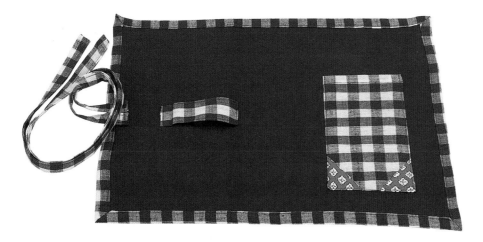

materials

Blue and white check for the casing: 18 x 18in/ 46 x 46cm

Solid blue for the lining: 16 x 11in/41 x 28cm

Green fabric scraps for the decoration

⬤ MADE IN A WEEKEND

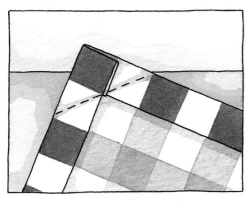

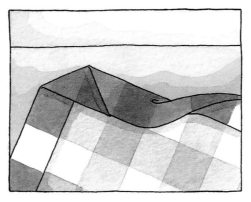

casing

1 Cut one blue and white check casing 16½ x 11¾in/42 x 29.75cm.

2 Turn in a ½in/1.5cm hem around the raw edge of the blue and white check. Press. Fold in the corner. Press.

3 Turn in another ½in/1.5cm hem. Press, then open out the folds. The second hem will create a neat mitre at each corner.

4 Trim away the corners to reduce bulk, just above the intersection of the pressed lines. (Practise on a spare scrap first.)

5 Fold in a small seam at the diagonal corner at the point of the intersection, then refold the hems.

lining
1 Cut one lining 15½ × 10¾in/39.5 × 27.25cm from solid blue.

2 Cut one pocket from blue and white check 4¾ × 7½in/12 × 19cm.

3 From green scraps, cut two triangles for the decoration at the bottom of the pocket. For a positional guide, place one triangle at each bottom corner of the pocket.

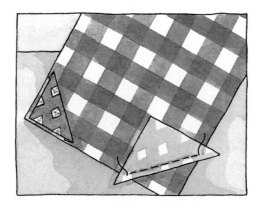

4 Flip the triangles over so that right sides are together and pin. Machine stitch each triangle decoration in place using a small seam allowance. Flip the triangles into the correct position and press flat.

5 Turn in a ½in/1.5cm seam allowance around the raw edge of the cutlery pocket. Overcast the raw edges to prevent fraying.

6 At the top edge turn in another ½in/1.5cm. Press and topstitch to finish.

7 Using the photograph of the placemat on page 55 as a guide, position the pocket on the lining and pin in place.

8 Try the knives and forks in the pocket and adjust to fit as necessary. You may need to make a pleat at the bottom edge.

9 Cut one piece of blue and white check 5 x 2¼in/12.75 x 5.75cm for the tab to hold the napkin in place. Turn in ½in/1.5cm around the raw edges. Press. Overcast the raw edges and machine stitch the fold. Pin and stitch in place on the lining.

10 Position the lining on the wrong side of the blue and white check so that the raw edges are encased.

ties

1 To make the ties, cut two pieces of check 2 x 21in/5 x 53.5cm.

2 Turn in the short edges and press. Fold in half lengthways and press. Open out the fold.

3 Turn in the long raw edges to the centre fold. Press, then refold on the centre foldline. Stitch the folded edges.

4 Centre the ties on the left-hand side edge of the lining. Stitch in place.

baguette holder

cutting

1 From blue and white check, cut one piece for the outer casing 15½ × 10½in/31.75 × 26.75cm. Cut one blue and white check tie, 21 × 2in/53.5 × 5cm.

2 From blue, cut one piece for the lining 16½ × 10½in/42 × 26.75cm.

tie

1 To make the tie, turn in ⅛in/0.75cm at each short end. Press. Fold the tie in half lengthways. Press. Open out the fold. Turn in the long raw edges to the centre pressed line. Press, then refold along the pressed centre line. Stitch around the folded edges.

bag

1 Place the lining and casing right sides together, with one 10½in/26.75cm edge aligned. Stitch in place.

2 Refold the panel right sides out, so that all raw edges are aligned and ⅝in/1.5cm of lining is visible at the stitched edge which will form the top of the bag. Press.

3 To make the channel through which the tie will be threaded, on the raw edges, at each side, mark with a pin 1½in/3.75cm from the top folded edge and 2½in/6.5cm from the top edge. Stitch each side of the channel.

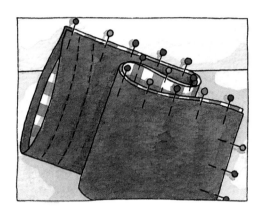

4 Fold the bag and lining in half so that the casing is on the inside and side raw edges are aligned.

5 Pin, aligning the checked pattern. Machine stitch the side and bottom bag seams, leaving the channel free of stitching.

6 Turn right side out. Press. Using the bodkin thread the tie through the channel to finish.

⏱ MADE IN AN HOUR

materials

Blue and white check:
22 × 15in/56 × 38cm

Blue for the lining:
22 × 15in/56 × 38cm

Sewing thread

Bodkin

stencilled garden bench

Spruce up your outdoor furniture with this old-fashioned paint technique. Stencilling is easy to master, quick to do and the simple shapes and bright colours are instantly appealing. Add a coat of varnish to weatherproof your work.

I Trace the watering can pattern provided. Transfer the tracing to the centre of the oiled stencil card.

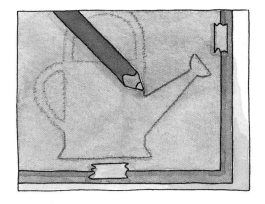

2 Cut out the watering can using the craft knife. Do not discard the handle inserts.

3 Determine the number of watering cans that will fit evenly spaced across the surface of the bench. Mark the position of each at the base and centre of each can.

4 Reposition the stencil on the bench and hold it and the handle inserts in position with spraymount glue.

5 Mix one part white with two parts colour. Fill in all the cans which face the same direction. Clean the stencil, then use the other side for the cans which face in the opposite direction. Allow to dry.

materials

Flat pack garden bench (this is much easier to stencil onto than a ready assembled seat)

Pelikan Plaka waterproof casein paint: blue, green and cream

White emulsion paint

Spraymount glue

Oiled stencil card and stencil brush

Craft knife

Tracing paper and pencil

Sponge

TEMPLATE: SEE PAGE 117

⏱ MADE IN A WEEKEND

6 Using the cut-out can shapes, cut away two stripes at the top and bottom of the can body.

7 Using cream paint, sponge through the cut out stripes.

8 When the paint is dry, treat the surface of the stencils with matt varnish.

The fruit crate was decorated in exactly the same way as the garden bench, this time using a smaller scale template.

garden bench cushion

FINISHED SIZE: 17 X 38IN/43.25 X 96.5CM
• ADAPT THE MEASUREMENTS TO FIT YOUR BENCH

1 From green stripe cut eight pieces 9 × 10in/23 × 25cm. Cut the same from green.

2 Arrange the squares into the cushion top and bottom – eight for each side – alternating the colourways.

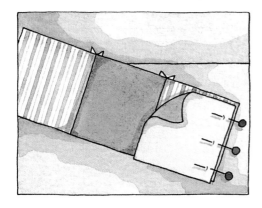

3 Stitch four pieces together into a row, then stitch two rows together.

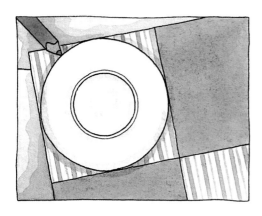

4 Using a plate and a fabric marker, at each corner, draw a curved corner. Cut out.

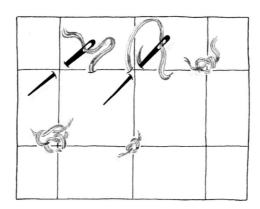

tie-quilting

1 The intersection of each square is decorated with tie quilting. Thread a needle with three lengths of green wool.

2 Beginning on the right side of the work insert the needle close to the intersection of four squares. Leave a 2–3in/5–7.5cm end of wool at the start.

3 Bring the needle out ⅛in/0.5cm away. Make a second stitch over the first.

4 Tie a square knot, first right over left, then left over right. Trim the thread ends to 1½in/3.75cm long.

5 For the side panel, from solid green, cut and piece a length 70 × 2½in/177.75 × 6.5cm.

6 For the panel surrounding the zip cut two solid green pieces 38½ × 2in/97.75 × 5cm.

materials

Green stripe: 1yd/1m

Solid green: 1yd/1m

Sewing thread

1½in/3.75cm-thick foam:
17 × 38in/43.25 × 96.5cm

Two zippers each 16in/41cm

Fabric marker

Green wool for the ties

Paper to make a pattern if required

⏱ MADE IN A WEEKEND

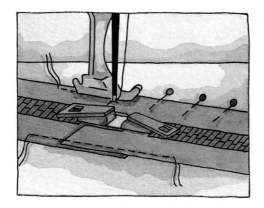

inserting the concealed zipper

1 Close the zippers. The tab ends of the two zippers touch. Overlap the fabric ends of the zipper, so that the two tabs meet, and stitch together using a zipper foot. The two halves of the zipper will open out from the centre towards the sides of the cushion. Set side.

2 Place the two solid green 38½in/97.75cm lengths right sides together with raw edges aligned. Baste one long edge.

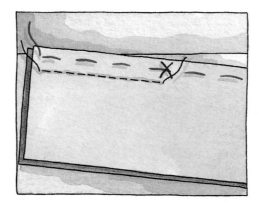

3 Centre the zipper on the basted long edge. On the solid green, mark with a coloured thread, the end of the zipper. Remove the zipper. Stitch each end of the solid green lengths together from the coloured thread to the short raw edges using ½in/1.5cm seam.

4 Press the seam open along the full length of the basted edge.

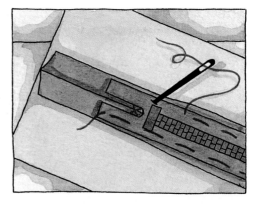

5 Replace the zipper over the basted opening so that it is right side down and centred over the opening. Baste in place.

6 Using a zipper foot, stitch the zipper in place without catching the teeth.

7 Reinforce the stitching over the point where the two zips overlap. Remove the basting stitches.

making up the cushion

1 Pin the zipper panel to one long edge of one cushion panel.

2 Find the centre of a long side of the remaining side panel.

3 Align the centre point with the centre of the remaining long edge of the cushion panel. Pin.

4 Pin the side panel to the cushion, right sides together, easing the fabric around the curved edges, without distorting or puckering the fabric.

5 The zipper panel and the side panel will overlap at the short edges. Pin the overlap.

6 Remove the side and zipper panels and stitch together the short ends at the overlap to form one continuous piece. Check the fit around the cushion. Trim the panel to the same width throughout.

7 Machine stitch the side panel to a patchwork cushion panel.

8 Pin the second cushion panel to the side panel. Stitch around three sides. Open the

zipper slightly, then stitch the remaining edge in place. Turn right side out through the zipper. Press carefully.

ties

1 Cut two ties from solid green 30 x 2½in/76.25 x 6.5cm.

2 Turn in ½in/1.5cm at each short end. Press. Fold the strip in half lengthways and press. Open out the fold. Turn in the long raw edges to the centre foldline and press. Refold on the centre foldline. Press, then machine stitch the edges.

3 Find the centre of each tie and mark with a pin.

4 Align each pin with each end of the zipper on the zipper panel or with the posts around which the tie will be knotted. Stitch the centre point to the panel.

5 To finish, insert the foam cushion pad.

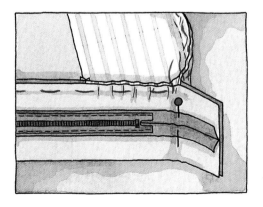

spongeware flower pots

Decorate terracotta plantpots with paint to match your interior decor.
Try printing first on scrap paper to achieve the desired density of colour.

1 Clean the pots thoroughly with soap and water and allow to dry.

2 In a clean palette, make a mix of paint using white emulsion combined with different shades. Add more colour until the required density is achieved.

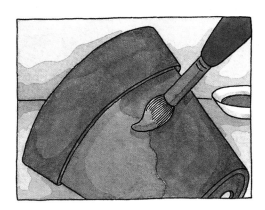

3 Paint the pots as desired. Allow to dry. Add a second coat.

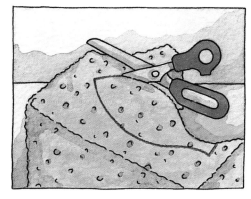

4 Draw your chosen motif on a sponge. Using scissors, accurately cut out each leaf and flower shape.

5 Mix stronger shades of the same colour of paint, this time using less white emulsion.

6 Dip the motif edge of the sponge in paint and test print onto a scrap of paper. When satisfied apply to the plant pot.

materials

Selection of terracotta plantpots

White emulsion paint

Selection of Plaka Pelican waterproof paint

Sponges

Paint brushes

Scissors

TEMPLATES: SEE PAGE 117

⚱ MADE IN AN AFTERNOON

painted glass lights

Glass lanterns provide soft lighting when entertaining outdoors. Glass paints are available in good craft stores and are easy to use. Simply paint an outline, then fill in the shapes.

materials

Selection of straight-sided glass jam jars and night light holders

Pebeo Vitrail stained glass outliner paint: transparent

Pebeo gold relief outliner: 'Cerne Relief'

A selection of Pelikan Plaka waterproof casein paints

Raffia, coloured string, twine or cord

Glass or wood beads

Container candles

MADE IN AN EVENING

1 Draw your chosen design onto the glass using outliner. Ensure that there are no breaks in the line of outliner and that the lines you paint are thick enough to act as a barrier to stop the main colours flooding through. Allow to set.

3 To make a hanging string, cut thread the required length. Onto each end knot a bead.

4 Cut a second length of thread and tie it around the neck of the jar, trapping the beads of the hanging string at each side.

2 Fill in with your choice of colours.

5 Place a candle inside each jar to finish.

THINGS FOR
A RAINY DAY

autumnal lap quilt

Use simple appliqué to embellish and transform a plain blanket into a stylish throw. Autumn leaves in warm seasonal colours are cut from templates and stitched in place with decorative embroidery.

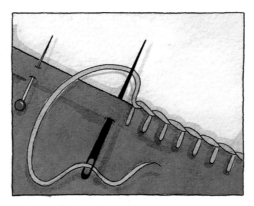

1 If the raw edges are unfinished, turn in a seam allowance to the wrong side and pin in place. Using a contrasting colour wool, blanket stitch the turned-in edge in place.

materials

Blanketing or polarfleece: 36 x 48in/91.5 x 122cm

Felt squares in gold, yellow, orange, various greens and red

Stranded wool in the same shades as above

Selection of leaves

Paper and paper scissors

Pinking shears

Pencil

Pins and needle with a large eye

TEMPLATES: SEE PAGES 118–119

⏱ MADE IN A WEEKEND

2 From your selection of leaves, or from the templates available, trace the leaf shapes on paper and cut out to make paper patterns.

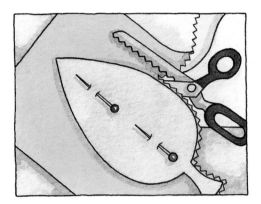

3 Pin each paper pattern to a square of felt and cut out with pinking shears.

4 Spread the blanketing or polarfleece on a flat surface. Arrange the felt leaves on top. When you are happy with the arrangement, replace the felt leaves with the paper ones for position only. Pin in place.

5 Starting with the centre leaves, exchange one paper leaf for a felt leaf and stitch down one at a time using a variety of different stitches. Work from the centre outwards. Use a contrast colour thread. Some leaves are applied with running stitch.

6 Return to each leaf and embellish each with couching and zigzag running stitch (see stitch illustrations below). Let the shape of each leaf dictate the stitches you choose. Use brightly coloured contrast threads and keep an even length stitch throughout.

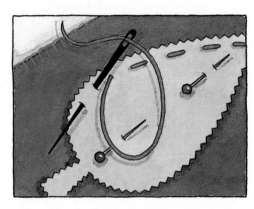

Running stitch

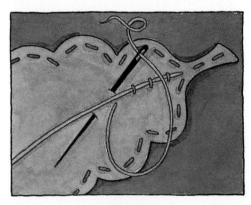

Couching

Zigzag stitch

autumn lampshade

Recycle an old lampshade by recovering the shade with handmade or unusual textured papers. Make a mock-up template first to determine the paper dimensions required.

1 Measure the circumference of the bottom of your shade, then measure the height. Cut a piece of brown paper or newspaper larger than your measurements — approximately 1in/2.5cm excess.

2 Wrap the paper around the shade, over-lapping where necessary to create a snug fit. Mark and trim the paper to fit, allowing sufficient for a seam to overlap at the back of the shade.

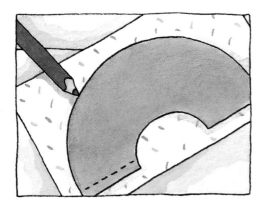

3 Use the newspaper shade as your template. Place it on top of your selected handmade paper. Draw lightly around it and cut out carefully.

4 Using spraymount adhesive, carefully stick the handmade paper shade over the old one, smoothing out any creases or air bubbles. Glue the seam for extra strength. Keep a damp cloth to hand to remove any excess glue. Allow to dry.

Hints

• Choose a lampshade with a simple shape.

• Wash old fabric shades first with fabric detergent and water.

• Allow to dry thoroughly or the adhesive will not stick.

materials

Brown paper or newspaper

A selection of handmade papers

Lampshade

Spraymount adhesive

PVA glue

Pencil and scissors

Neutral colour webbing tape 1in/2.5cm wide

Orange string

Cardboard and tracing paper for templates

TEMPLATES: SEE PAGE 119

⏱ MADE IN A DAY

5 To apply the webbing to the top of the shade, begin at the seam.

6 Apply adhesive to the webbing. Allow to dry slightly, then stick in place so that the webbing covers the raw edge of the paper, goes over the edge and inside the shade. Pull the webbing taut as you work, without distorting the webbing. Glue as you go and smooth the webbing into the inside of the shade with a cloth.

7 Repeat at the bottom edge. Then apply a contrast trim using PVA glue.

8 Trace the templates from the patterns provided. Stick the tracings to thin cardboard and cut out.

9 Using the templates, cut leaf motifs from a selection of handmade papers.

10 Apply spray mount glue to the back of the leaves and apply each to the shade. Glue and apply six at a time.

11 For the blue button shade, make the shade in the same way following steps 1–10. Adhere buttons to the top and bottom rims.

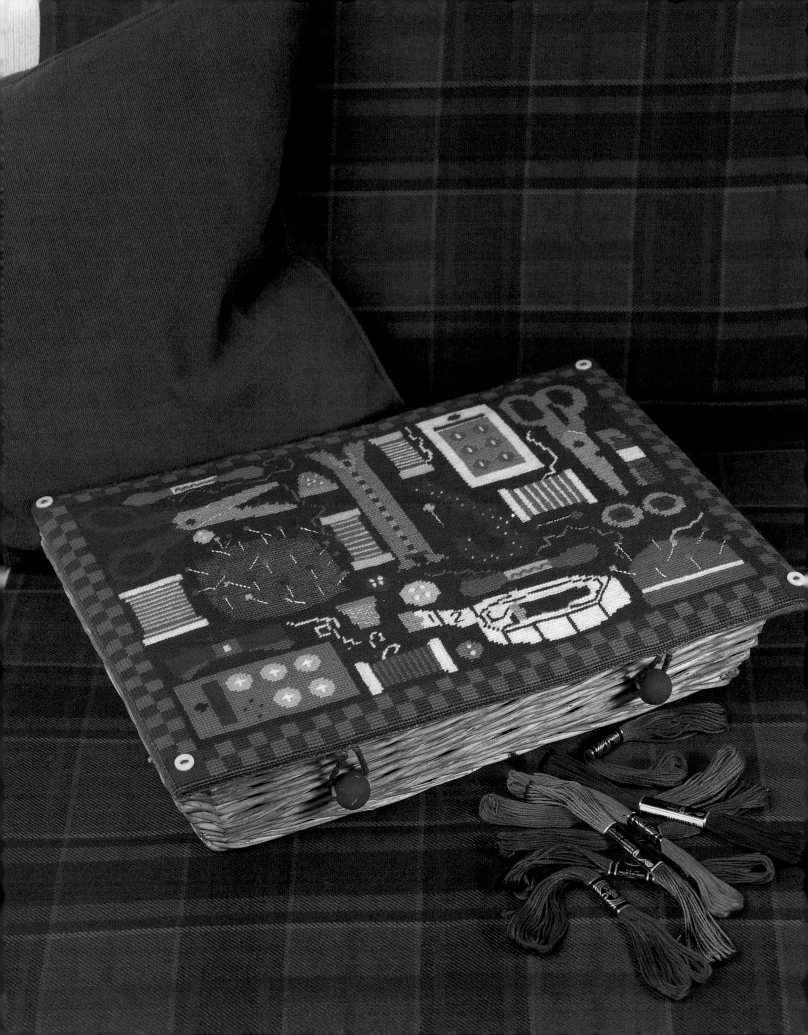

needlepoint sewing box

Convert a wicker cutlery holder into a box and add a needlepoint lid for an instant sewing box. Worked in simple half-cross stitch, the pattern can be adapted to fit any size box, by simply amending the border.

15½ X 11½IN/39.5 X 29.25CM

materials

FOR THE NEEDLEWORK BOX LID:

14 hpi tapestry canvas

½yd/0.5m

DMC shade	Colour Key	No of skeins
7017	Purple	9
7947	Orange	4
7030	Blue	3
7544	Red	2
7153	Pink	1
7021	Grey	1
7018	Lilac	1
7037	Turquoise	1
7914	Dark green	2
7911	Bright green	1
7971	Yellow	2
1535	Ecru	2
1410	Rayon thread	1
4 small buttons		

1 Enlarge the template provided on page 120–121 on a photocopier by 125%.

2 Transfer the pattern onto the centre of the tapestry canvas. To do this it may help if you have access to a lightbox or stick the design to a window and hold the canvas over the top. Then retrace the design lines onto the canvas.

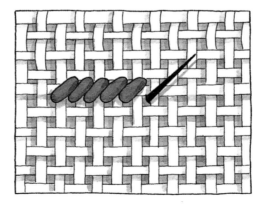

3 Fill in the colours using the chart as your guide and working in half cross stitch.

4 Stretch the finished work (see overleaf). Add a button to each corner.

🕐 WILL TAKE MORE THAN A MONTH

materials

FOR THE BOX:

Thick cardboard:

11 x 15in/28 x 38cm

Blue for backing fabric
½yd/0.5m

Wadding: ½yd/0.5m

Double-sided tape

Sewing cotton

Strong thread

Basket box: approximately

11 x 15 x 3in/28 x 38 x 7.5cm

Pins

Braid

Two Large beads for
fasteners

finishing

1 Cut two pieces of wadding the same size as the box lid. Tape to the cardboard.

2 Trim the canvas 2in/5cm larger all around than the needlepoint design.

3 Centre the needlework on one side of the wadding. Turn to the back. Fold the excess canvas around the cardboard at two opposite sides. Pin temporarily in place.

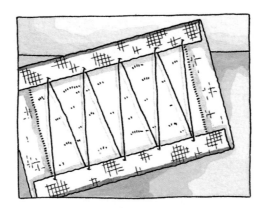

4 With strong thread, lace backwards and forwards across the width, stretching the canvas taut over the cardboard.

Hints

• To stretch distorted needlework back into shape, make a wooden frame the size of the required finished needlework.

• Tack one side of the design to the wooden frame below. With a mist spray, dampen the surface of the needlework. Do not saturate the work.

• Gently pull the work into shape, anchoring the sides with tacks. Allow to dry.

5 Turn in the two remaining ends of canvas and repeat.

6 Make the two loops to fasten the lid to the base by twisting 5in/13cm lengths of blue and orange thread together. Secure the loops to the underside of the box with a few stitches.

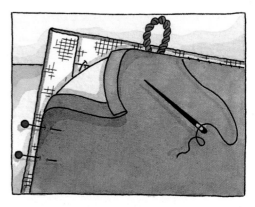

7 Cut a piece of fabric to fit the back of the lid, adding a ½in/1.5cm seam allowance all around. Turn in the seam allowance and press carefully.

8 Hand stitch the backing to the turned in edges of canvas, so that the fabric joins onto the dark green border and the canvas is not visible. Make your stitches as neat and as invisible as possible.

9 Paint the basket blue.

10 Attach the bead fasteners to the basket using raffia.

11 Attach the lid to the basket with raffia hinges. Stitch through the lid lining and through the holes in the basketry. Knot the raffia on the inside of the basket.

painted leaf cushions

Minimal sewing skills are required to make these two autumnal cushion covers. The appliqué decoration is made separately by painting onto linen and is applied to the background using time-saving fusible web.

FINISHED SIZE 14½ X 14½IN/37 X 37CM

appliqué decoration

1 Trace the leaf templates provided. Stick the tracing to thin cardboard. Accurately cut out each shape.

2 Depending on your choice of cushion, cut either one or four squares of natural Cashel linen 4 x 4in/10 x 10cm for the cushion front appliqué decoration.

3 Fray ¼in/0.75cm of the raw edges all around each square.

4 With a pencil, lightly draw around the leaf templates on the right side of the natural linen squares.

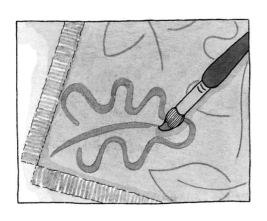

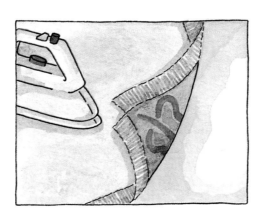

5 Paint the outline of the leaves using different shades of fabric paint. Allow to dry.

6 Fill in the shapes using yellow. When the paint is dry, iron the wrong side of the linen to fix the dyes.

7 Add any embroidery details.

8 Cut squares of fusible web 3½ x 3½in/ 9 x 9cm and bond one square to the wrong side of painted linen. Put to one side.

cushion

1 From blue linen, for the cushion front, cut one square 15½ x 15½in/39.25 x 39.25cm.

materials

Blue DMC Cashel linen: ½yd/0.5m

Green DMC Cashel linen: ½yd/0.5m

Natural Cashel linen: scraps for the tab fastener and appliqué decoration

Scraps of fusible web

One self-cover button ⅞in/2.25cm in diameter

Marabu fabric paints: red, brown, green and yellow

Pencil, tracing paper and cardboard

Sewing thread

TEMPLATES: SEE PAGE 123

⌚ MADE IN A WEEKEND

2 Fuse the appliqué decoration to the centre front of the blue linen square. Hand stitch in place.

3 From green linen, for the cushion back, cut one piece 15½ x 12in/39.25 x 30.5cm, and one piece 15½ x 11in/39.25 x 28cm.

4 From blue linen scraps, cover one button following the manufacturer's instructions.

5 Cut one tab from neutral linen, 1 x 7½in/ 2.5 x 19cm. Turn in a ¼in/0.75cm seam at the short ends. Press. Fold the tab in half lengthways wrong sides together. Press. Open out the fold. Fold in the long raw edges to the centre fold. Press, then refold on the centre line. Stitch the edges of the tab. Put aside.

6 Turn in ½in/1.5cm on one 15½in/39.25cm edge of each green cushion back. Press. Turn in another 2½in/6.5cm on the same edge.

7 Fold the tab into a loop and position on the wrong side of the larger green piece. Pin in place. Topstitch the pressed edge of the back, catching in the tab as you sew. Topstitch the pressed edge of the second back piece.

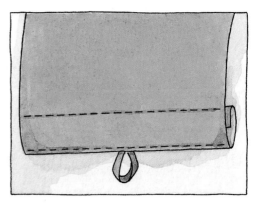

8 Overlap the stitched edges of the two halves of the cushion back, to measure 15½in/39.25cm square. The piece with the tab should be underneath. Baste the overlap.

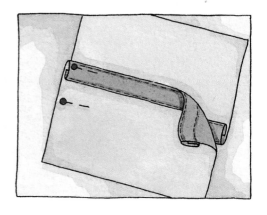

9 With right sides together, place the cushion back on the cushion front. Pin. Stitch together using a ½in/1.5cm seam. Turn right side out. Add a button to finish.

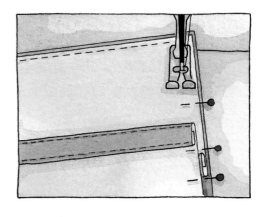

knitted drawstring bag

Knitting and purling and the ability to follow a chart are the only skills needed for this drawstring bag. The lining is hand-stitched in place and the bag is finished with a plaited braid.

FINISHED SIZE 8 X 10½IN/20.25 X 26.75CM

materials

Rowan Donegal lambswool tweed 4-ply knitting yard in the following shades and quantities:

Navy: 4oz/100gms
Small amount of leaf green
Small amount of salmon
Small amount of pale blue
Small amount of chocolate brown
Cream bouclé or textured yarn for the sheep
Two beads for the eyes
Red flannel: ¼yd/0.25m
Bodkin
One pair knitting needles

⏱ MADE IN A WEEK

tension

Using US10/UK3¼mm needles, 26 stitches and 34 rows measures 4in/10cm.

back

Using main colour, cast on 56 stitches. Work in stocking stitch until work measures 11¼in/28.5cm, ending on a wrong side row (slip the first stitch of each row for a more even appearance at the edges). Cast off loosely and evenly.

front

1 Repeat as for back, until work measures 4in/10cm, ending with a wrong side row.

2 Knit 10, then joining in yarn and working from chart, pattern 36, at the same time, carrying and twisting in the main colour across the back of the work, then knit 10 in main colour.

3 Continue working from the chart, joining in new colours as required until all 40 rows of the chart are complete. Maintain an even tension throughout.

4 Continue in main colour until work measures 11¼in/28.5cm, ending on a wrong side row. Cast off loosely and evenly.

finishing

1 Sew in all the loose ends. Press the wrong side of the work using a damp cloth and ensuring work does not distort.

2 Press in ½in/1.5cm at top of work to give a neat folded edge.

3 Stitch on two beads for the sheep's eyes.

4 To make the lining, measure the work and cut two pieces of red flannel ½in/1.5cm larger all around. Turn in a seam allowance all around and press.

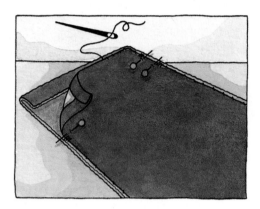

5 With wrong sides together, slipstitch a lining to the bag back and front. Leave a ½in/1.5cm wide gap 1in/2.5cm from the folded bag top.

6 Reinforce the machine stitching at each side of the gap.

7 Baste, then machine stitch a ½in/1.5cm-wide channel, 1in/2.5cm and 1½in/3.75cm from the top folded edge to clear the gap made at steps 5 and 6.

8 Place the knitted bag front and back right sides together.

9 Stitch the sides and bottom together, leaving a gap for the braid handle to be threaded through.

braid

1 Cut 18 strands of wool, each 1yd/1m long. Separate into three groups of six strands and knot one end of each group.

2 Tie the lengths to a fixed point, then tightly plait the strands, then knot the ends together. Trim the loose ends.

3 Using a dress-makers bodkin, thread the braid through the channel. Knot the two ends together.

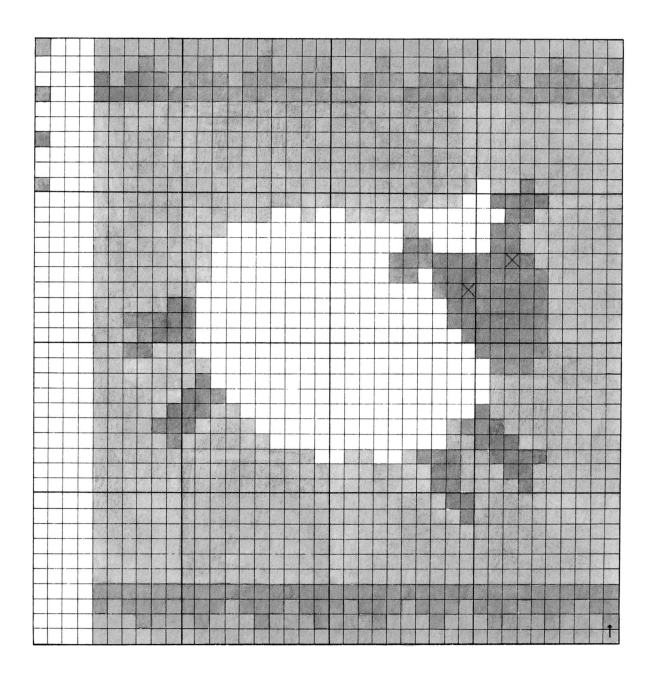

key

leaf green	⬜
salmon	🟫
pale blue	🟦
chocolate brown	🟫
cream bouclé	⬜
beads	⊠

album cover

This attractive rainy day scrap album cover is made of textured handmade paper and pressed leaves mounted onto corrugated board. This novel method includes a waxed paper technique.

FINISHED SIZE 13 X 17½ X 1IN/33 X 44.5 X 2.5CM

pressed leaf decoration

1 Collect a selection of attractive leaves. Ensure each is dry, then press between sheets of blotting paper inside the leaves of a thick, heavy book.

2 Place a sheet of waxed paper, wax side up on an ironing board. Arrange the pressed leaves on the surface, ensuring there is plenty of space around each. Place a second sheet of waxed paper, wax side down over the leaves, ensuring that the leaves do not shift.

3 Place a piece of fabric such as a tea towel over the waxed paper and press with a hot dry iron. Experiment first with different temperatures. The heat of the iron should

bond the waxed paper and the leaves together. If the iron is too hot the wax will simply disappear. Allow to cool.

4 Roughly cut the waxed paper into 2in/5cm squares, so that the leaf is centred in the square. Put to one side.

5 For the yellow squares behind the leaves, using a pencil and ruler, very lightly draw nine squares each 2¾in/7cm onto the paper.

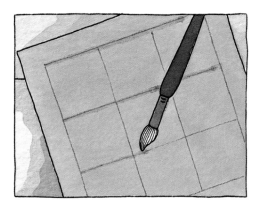

6 Dip a fine paint brush in water and paint along the drawn line. While the paper is still wet, carefully 'tear' along the drawn line. The effect will be slightly ragged as a deckle edge. Allow to dry.

materials

A selection of fresh or pressed leaves

Blotting paper

Pencil and paint brush

Sheets of unusual, textured or hand made paper

Waxed paper and an iron

Embroidery thread

Brown corrugated board: 34 x 23¾in/86.5 x 60.5cm

Neutral linen: ½yd/0.5m

Scraps of dark linen

Spraymount glue

Double-sided tape

Fusible web: ½yd/0.5m

1in/2.5cm wide webbing tape: 1½yd/1.5m

TEMPLATE: SEE PAGE 122

⏱ MADE IN A WEEKEND

7 Centre the waxed paper leaf on the yellow square and stitch the two together with a French knot at each corner.

album

1 Transfer the album cover dimensions given on page 122 to the corrugated board.

2 Define the foldlines by creasing on the inner drawn lines.

3 Measure the front and back of the album and cut two pieces of textured paper 2in/5cm longer and 1in/2.5cm wider.

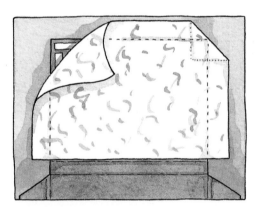

4 Using spraymount glue and double-sided tape where appropriate, stick the paper in place, aligning one long edge with the spine, so that the overlap is at the top, bottom and inside jacket. Fold in the two corners.

5 Glue to the folded edge, then fold in or stick down the head, foot and inside edge.

6 Cut two pieces of paper slightly smaller than the inside album dimensions. Stick in place on the inside front and inside back using glue or tape.

7 Make paper templates of the three flaps and their spines.

8 Cut each shape from linen slightly larger than the template for the outer cover.

9 Cut each shape the same size as the template for the inside album cover.

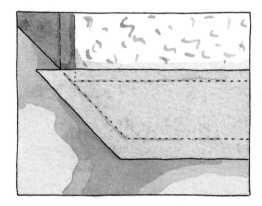

10 Stick the larger linen pieces to the outside of the album first, turn the excess to the inside. Stick the smaller pieces to the inside using double-sided tape.

11 Cut one length of dark linen slightly longer than the height of the book and the spine width plus 4in/10cm.

12 Fray the long edges, then add running stitch decoration.

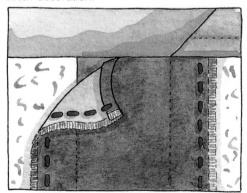

13 Turn under the short ends and press. (It may help to add strips of fusible web to the hem.) Stick the spine decoration in place so that it covers the paper edges.

14 Cut a second length of dark linen 2in/5cm wide and the height of the album. Stick in place on the inside spine.

15 From dark linen, cut two squares each 4in/10cm. Fray the edges and add a running stitch detail.

16 Place the top left corner of the linen over the bottom right corner of the album. Stick in place. Wrap the linen around into the inside of the album and stick in place. Trim the bottom edge of the linen, allowing a small seam to turn in to the inside. Repeat at the top edge.

17 Cut four dark linen squares each 3½in/9cm. Fray the edges and add running stitch detail. Bond a small scrap of fusible web to the centre of the wrong side of each.

18 Cut the webbing tape into four equal lengths. Cut a small slit in the centre of the dark linen square. (The fusible web will ensure the linen does not fray.) Thread one end of the webbing tape through the slit in the right side of the square and fuse in place on the wrong side.

19 Stick the squares in position and set on point. Use the plan as a guide. The webbing tape will tie to hold the contents of the scrap album securely in place. To finish, stick the leaf decorations in place.

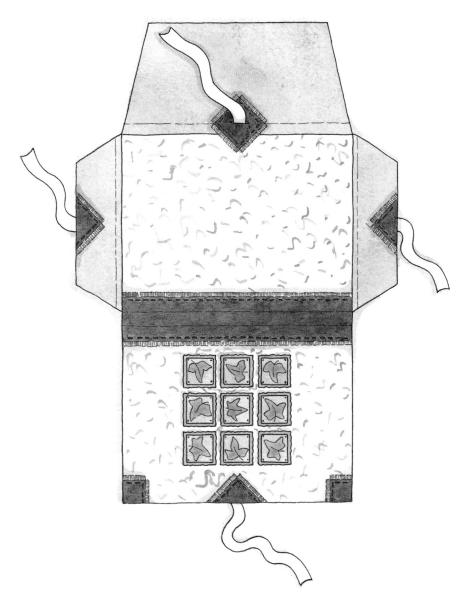

SEASONAL CHEER

christmas wreath

Use the soft-wood foundation of this example to make different festive wreaths to hang around the house. Decorated with cinnamon sticks and seasonal foliage, this wreath looks and smells attractive.

1 Twist several stems into a wreath, tying the lengths together at regular intervals.

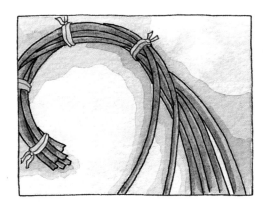

materials

Bundles of cinnamon

Raffia

Fresh ivy

Soft wood twigs such as willow to make the wreath

Florist's scissors

4 To make the cinammon star, arrange each cinammon stick following the diagram (right) and tying with raffia to secure the ends together. Tie the star, tassels and cinnamon bundles to the wreath.

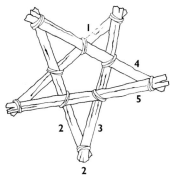

2 Tie cinnamon sticks together using raffia.

3 Make raffia tassels by wrapping around three fingers. Remove the bundle. Wrap a length of raffia tightly around the tassel neck. Seal with adhesive. Trim the other end.

🕐 MADE IN AN EVENING

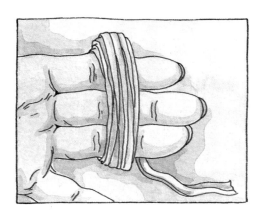

5 Make a raffia hanging loop. To finish wind fresh ivy or your choice of seasonal foliage around the wreath.

dough decorations

Children will enjoy making, baking and painting decorations to hang on the tree. Cookie cutters will provide the inspiration for the shapes. Practise making the dough to the correct thickness to hang on the tree without bending the boughs.

1 Trace the patterns provided. Stick the tracing to cardboard. Cut out.

2 Put the salt, flour and 1tbsp oil together in a bowl. Add small quantities of water at a time and mix together to a dough-like consistency. Knead well.

3 Roll out the dough to a ¼in/0.75cm thickness on a lightly floured surface. Using the templates or cutters, cut the required number of shapes.

4 Using a skewer, make a small hole at the top of each shape through which to thread the hanging string.

5 Using oil, lightly grease a baking tray. Bake the dough slowly in the middle of the oven at a low temperature for 1½ hours. The dough should sound hollow when tapped. Allow to cool.

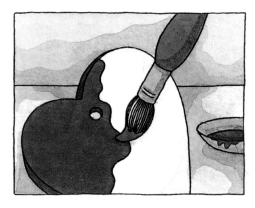

6 Paint as desired, allow to dry. Glue buttons or decoration to the front of the shapes.

materials

Salt: 10oz/300gm

Plain flour: 10oz/300gm

Oil: 2tbsp

Water to mix

Tracing paper, thin cardboard, pencil and sharp knife or use Christmas cookie cutters, skewer, PVA glue

Paints, paint brush

Buttons, beads, raffia, ribbon to decorate

TEMPLATES: SEE PAGE 123

⏱ MADE IN A WEEKEND

☺ SUITABLE FOR A CHILD TO MAKE

7 To make a hanging string, thread a length of raffia or paper string through the hole. Add beads for decoration over both strands. Knot to secure the bead in place.

angel peg dolly

These adorable little peg dolls are made from the smallest scraps of fabric, old-fashioned wooden pegs and paint – all materials to be found around the house. This project is so simple, it's an ideal way to involve children in the Christmas preparations.

materials

FOR EACH DOLLY YOU WILL NEED

One wooden peg

Fabric for the dress:

9 x 4in/23 x 10cm

1in/2.5cm-wide ribbon:

9in/23cm

PVA glue

A selection of beads, button, embroidery threads and paints in a variety of colours

Fine paint brushes

☺ SUITABLE FOR A CHILD TO MAKE

⌚ MADE IN A DAY

1 Paint the legs of the peg with a bright colour base. Allow to dry. Add spots or stripes in a contrast colour.

2 Paint on a face.

3 For the hair, cut short lengths of thread. Using glue, stick the strands to the top of the peg to form a fringe, then down the back of the head. Trim.

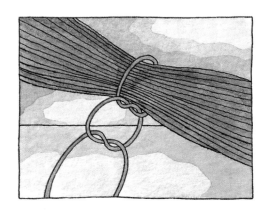

4 Collect a bundle of threads together for the sides of the hair. Make a knot around the centre with another thread and stick in place on top of the head.

5 Carefully thread another length of embroidery cotton under the knot, add beads and buttons and knot each in place. Tie the thread ends together to form the hanging thread.

6 To make the dress, with right sides together, stitch the 4in/10cm edges of the dress fabric together to make a tube.

7 Turn in ½in/1.5cm at the raw edges. Press.

8 Decorate the bottom edge of the dress with running stitch.

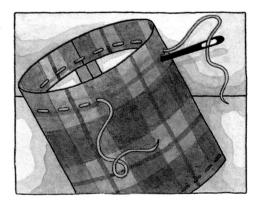

9 Beginning at the centre front, work gathering stitches around the top of the dress with a contrast embroidery thread.

10 Pull up the threads tight to fit the circumference of the peg and fit just below the face. Tie the thread ends in a bow at the front of the dress. Add your choice of beads to the thread ends.

11 To make the wings, fold the short ends of the ribbon in to the centre. Stitch in place, wrong sides together, then stitch the wings to the back of the dress.

printed boxes, tissue paper, gift tags, cards and bags

Customise your own Christmas wrapping with these seasonal potato print boxes, gift tags, paper carriers and boxes. The technique is simple and the results are guaranteed to be unique.

I Trace the templates provided. Stick the tracings to thin cardboard and cut out each.

2 Cut potatoes in half and hold the template to the cut section.

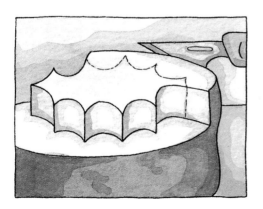

3 Carefully cut around the template or cut your own choice of shape by eye. Cut away the excess potato.

4 Dip the potato printing block in paint and print onto your selected tissue papers, blanks and greeting cards.

materials

Cardboard box blanks

Blank cards

Brown paper for the bags

Blank gift tags

Selection of papers

Tracing paper, cardboard, pencil

Raffia

Paint: red, green, white

Potatoes

Sharp knife

Pencil with eraser end

TEMPLATES: SEE PAGE 124–125

⏱ MADE IN AN EVENING

5 To make the berries, use the eraser end of the pencil, dipped in paint.

paper carrier bags

1 Decorate your choice of paper with motifs as desired. Allow to dry.

2 Enlarge the pattern provided on page 124 to the required dimensions. Transfer the pattern onto your decorated papers and cut out the shape. Define the foldlines.

3 Assemble the bag, following the instructions on page 25 and adhering the surfaces where appropriate.

christmas banner

For those who like sewing, this project offers the opportunity to stitch with different thread weights and textures. The heavier threads are simply wound by hand onto the spool, and are placed in the machine below the foot. The standard sewing cotton in the top of the machine keeps the tension even.

1 Bond fusible web to the wrong side of the fabric scraps.

2 Make templates from the patterns provided, by tracing off the shape, cutting out, then gluing to cardboard.

3 Place the templates on the paper side of the fusible web and draw around each. Cut the required number of shapes on the exact pencil lines.

4 Pink the raw edges of the felt pieces. Fold each in half. Press.

5 Position each motif on the felt, ensuring the folded edge is at the top. Position those motifs which are overlapped first.

6 Remove the paper backing from the wrong side of the shapes. Fuse each in place following the manufacturer's instructions.

materials

12 felt pieces:

8½ × 3½in/21.5 × 9cm

A selection of fabric scraps with small scale designs

Scraps of fusible web

Beads and buttons

Embroidery thread

Thin cardboard and tracing paper

Paper string

Bodkin

Sewing cotton

TEMPLATES: SEE PAGE 125

☙ MADE IN AN EVENING

7 Open out the felt. Add embroidery decoration and any buttons or beads. Refold the felt.

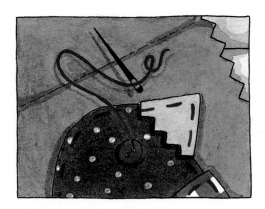

8 Machine stitch the front and back of the felt together, leaving sufficient space near the fold to thread string through. Wind the spool with embroidery thread. Put a contrast colour in the top of the machine and stitch the back and front together.

9 Make a banner by threading the felt pieces onto paper string.

CHRISTMAS CANDLES

candle wreaths

Glowing candles reflect the spirit of Christmas and no festive home is complete without them. They can be decorated in a multitude of ways and below are just two suggestions of how a simple candle can be transformed into a rich and evocative centrepiece.

materials

White beeswax candles

Pinecones

Walnuts

Almonds

Hazelnuts

Hot glue gun

Cardboard

🕯 MADE IN AN AFTERNOON

1 Gather together a selection of seasonal nuts and pinecones.

2 Cut a cardboard ring to size.

3 Arrange the pinecones around the candle base and stick together using a hot glue gun.

4 Glue on any additional decorations.

terracotta candle containers

materials

Assorted-size flowerpots

Skein natural-coloured raffia

Fresh cranberries

Red embroidery thread

Soft sand

⏱ MADE IN AN AFTERNOON

1 Refer to the instructions for the Christmas wreath on page 95 to make raffia tassels.

2 Wrap raffia around the rim of the pot. Glue in place. Add a tassel to cover the join.

3 Stick the candle to the base of the pot and fill with sand to three-quarters full.

4 Arrange a selection of cranberries around the sides of the candle.

easter tea cosy
Actual size
Add ½in/1.5cm seam
allowance all around for
the casing and lining.
Cut 2.

Cut 2 butterfly shapes
for the **easter tea cosy** top decoration.

Actual size
Motifs for the back of the **easter tea cosy**.
Choose any motifs for the napkin, napkin rings and placemat.

egg cosies
Cut 2 for each shape.

egg cosies

Actual size

Cut 2 for each shape.

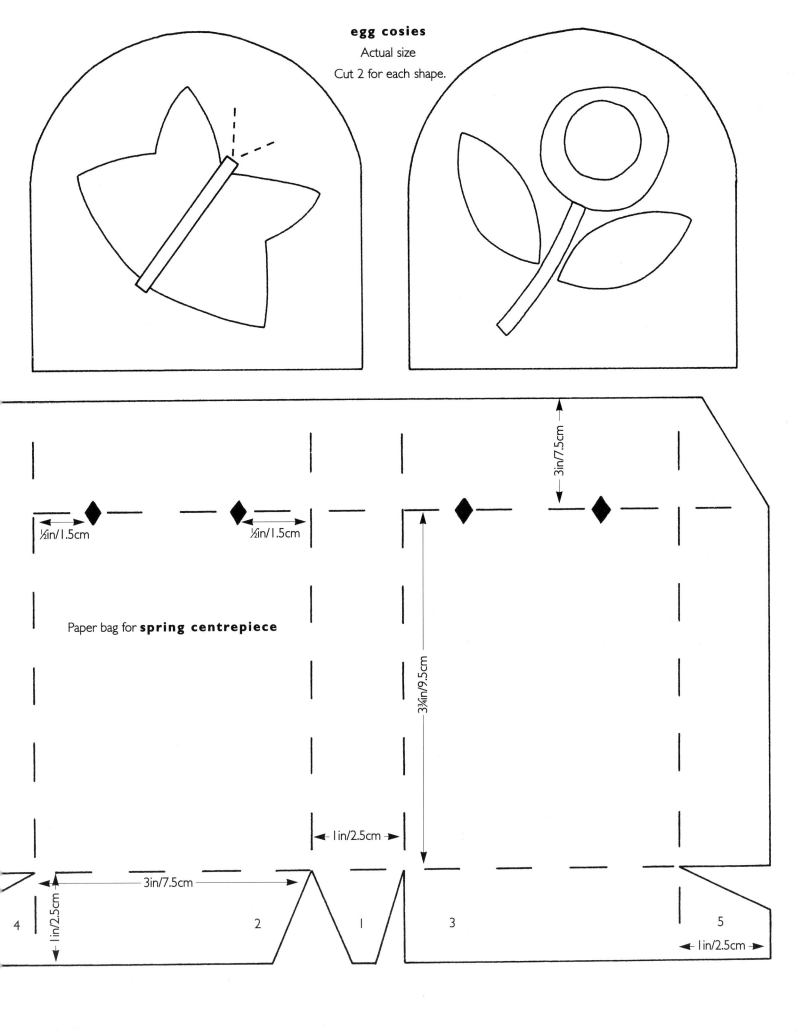

Paper bag for **spring centrepiece**

½in/1.5cm

½in/1.5cm

3in/7.5cm

3¾in/9.5cm

1in/2.5cm

3in/7.5cm

1in/2.5cm

1in/2.5cm

4

2

1

3

5

Actual size

gift tag

Alternate fish motifs

greeting card

spring centrepiece
Flower for Posy

spring centrepiece
Leaf for Posy

spring centrepiece Trug Border

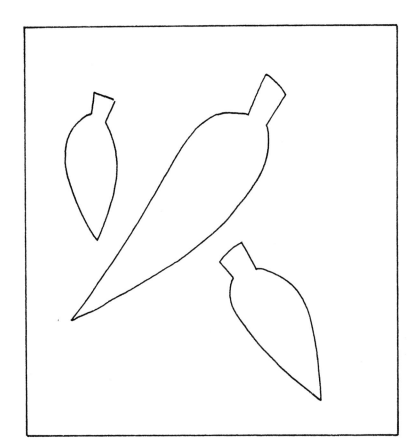

herb sachets

Actual size

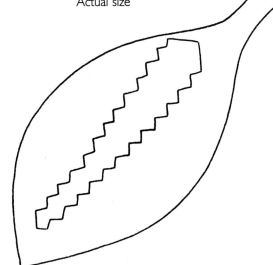

herb bags

113

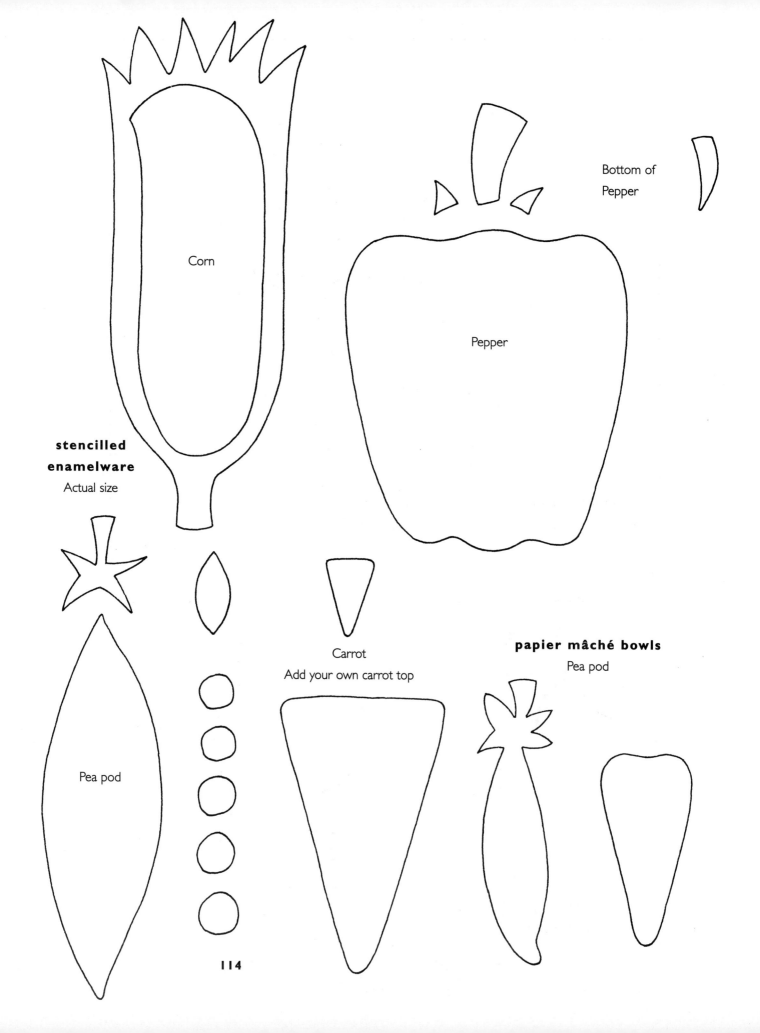

Corn

Bottom of
Pepper

Pepper

**stencilled
enamelware**

Actual size

Carrot

Add your own carrot top

papier mâché bowls

Pea pod

Pea pod

114

painted kitchen tile

Actual size

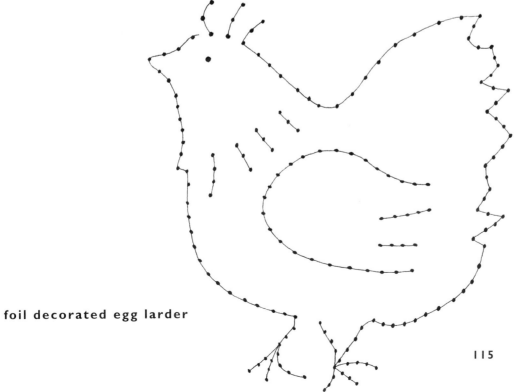

foil decorated egg larder

115

bird house

Actual size

Cut 1 base

Cut 2 sides

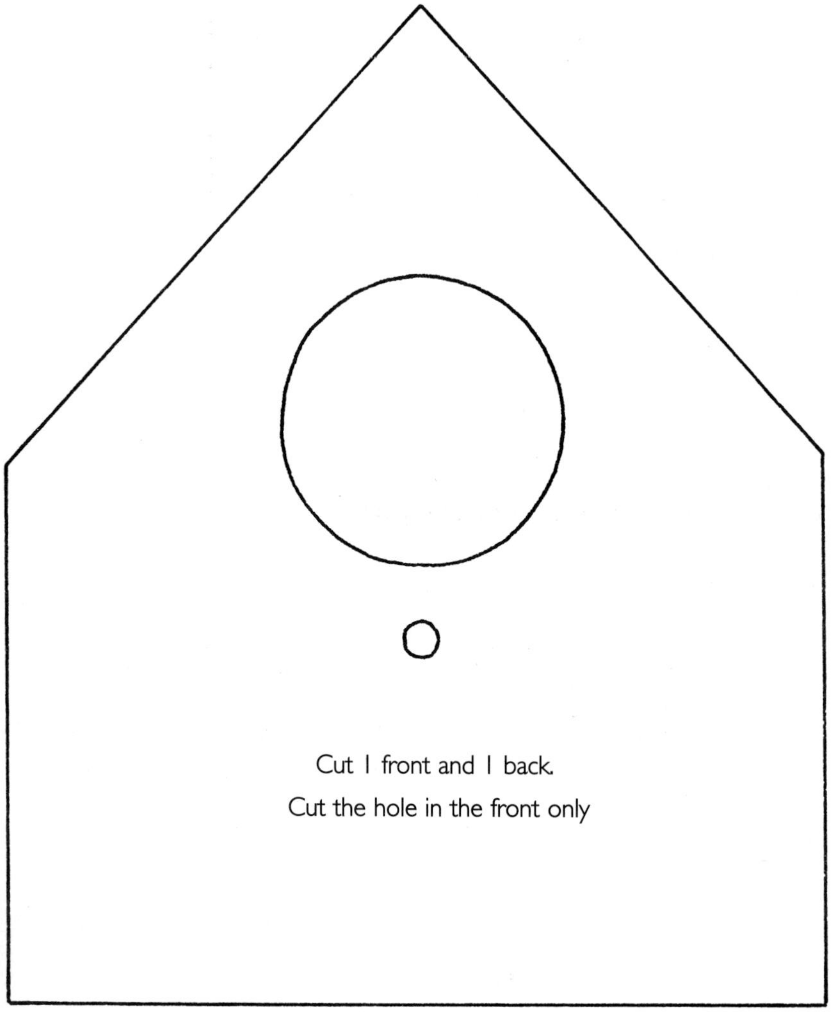

Cut 2 roof panels

Cut 1 front and 1 back.

Cut the hole in the front only

Bird stencil

stencilled garden bench

Actual size

Enlarge or reduce to fit the dimensions of your bench.

spongeware flower pots

autumnal lap quilt
Actual size

autumnal lap quilt

Actual size

autumn lampshade

Actual size

sewing box

Enlarge by 125%

The design is worked in half cross-stitch

Colour	DMC
Red	7544
Pink	7153
Purple	7017
Lilac	7021
Grey	7018
Blue	7030
Turquoise	7037
Dark Green	7914
Emerald Green	7911
Ecru	1535
Yellow	7971
Orange	7947

Silver thread for backstitch – pins, definition on scissors, French knots and trellis work on the thimbles

Colour pin heads using a variety of colours

The chequered border is worked in alternate squares of blue and orange

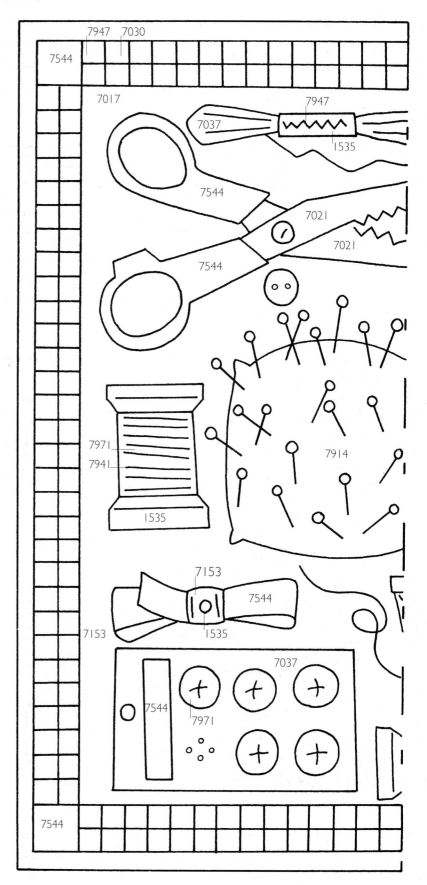

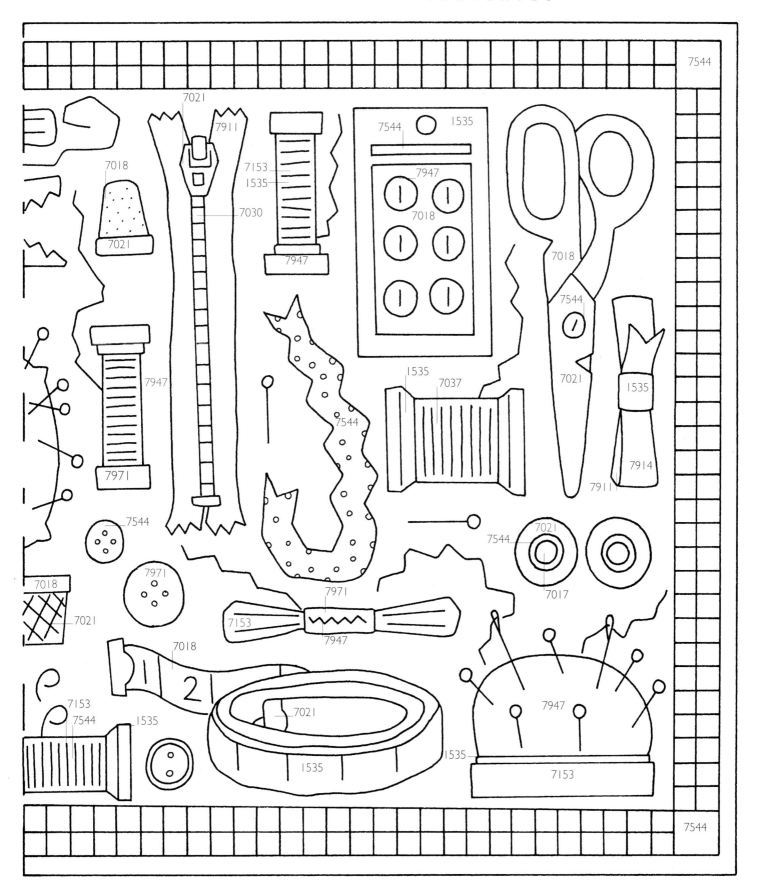

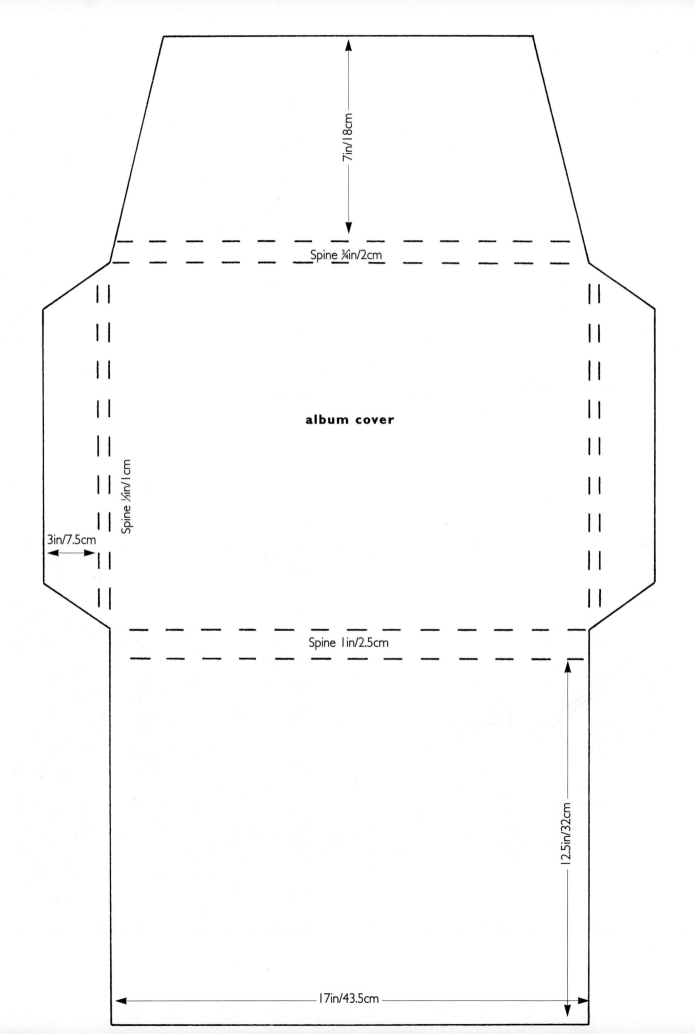

7in/18cm

Spine ¾in/2cm

album cover

Spine ⅜in/1cm

3in/7.5cm

Spine 1in/2.5cm

12.5in/32cm

17in/43.5cm

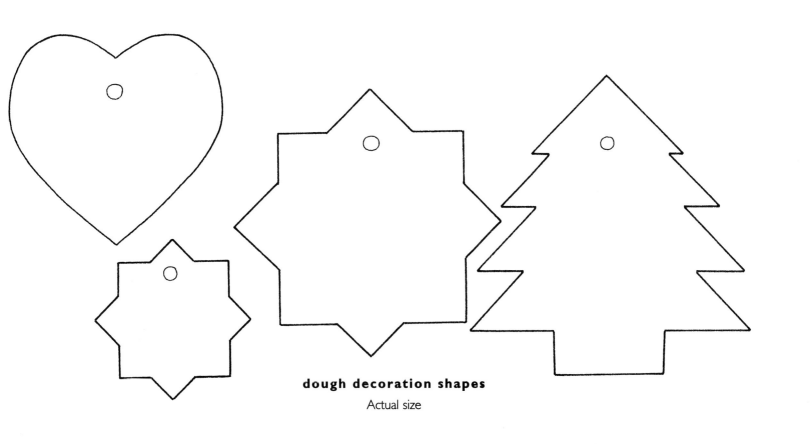

dough decoration shapes

Actual size

painted leaf cushions

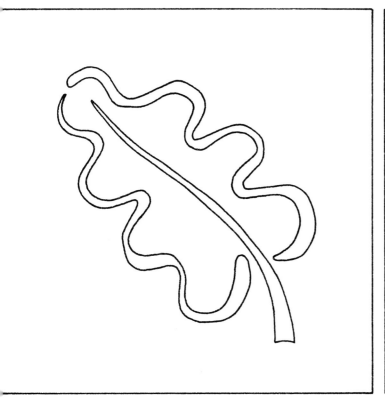

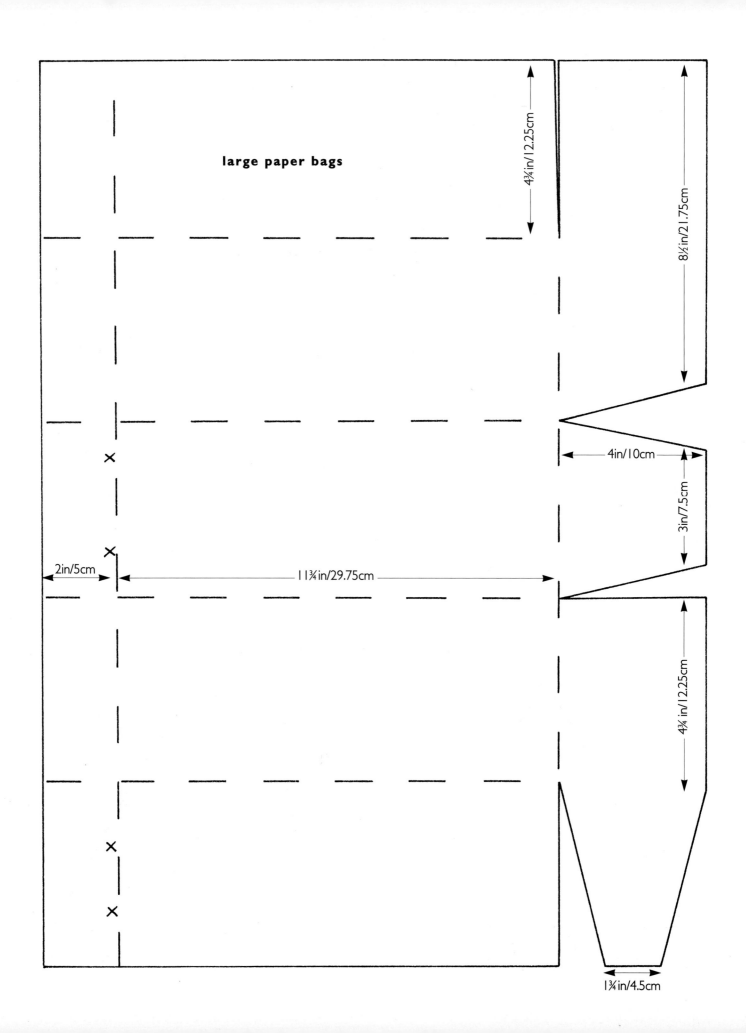

large paper bags

4¾in/12.25cm

8½in/21.75cm

4in/10cm

3in/7.5cm

2in/5cm

11¾in/29.75cm

4¾in/12.25cm

1¾in/4.5cm

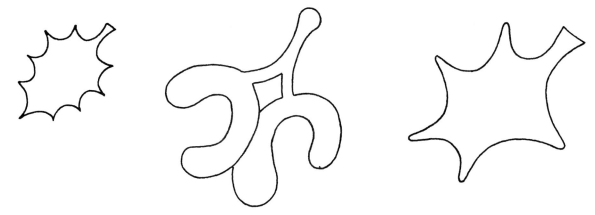

Motifs for the **christmas gift decorations**
Actual size

Motifs for the **christmas banner**
Actual size

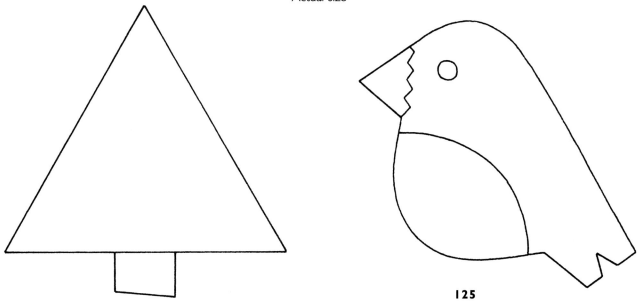

125

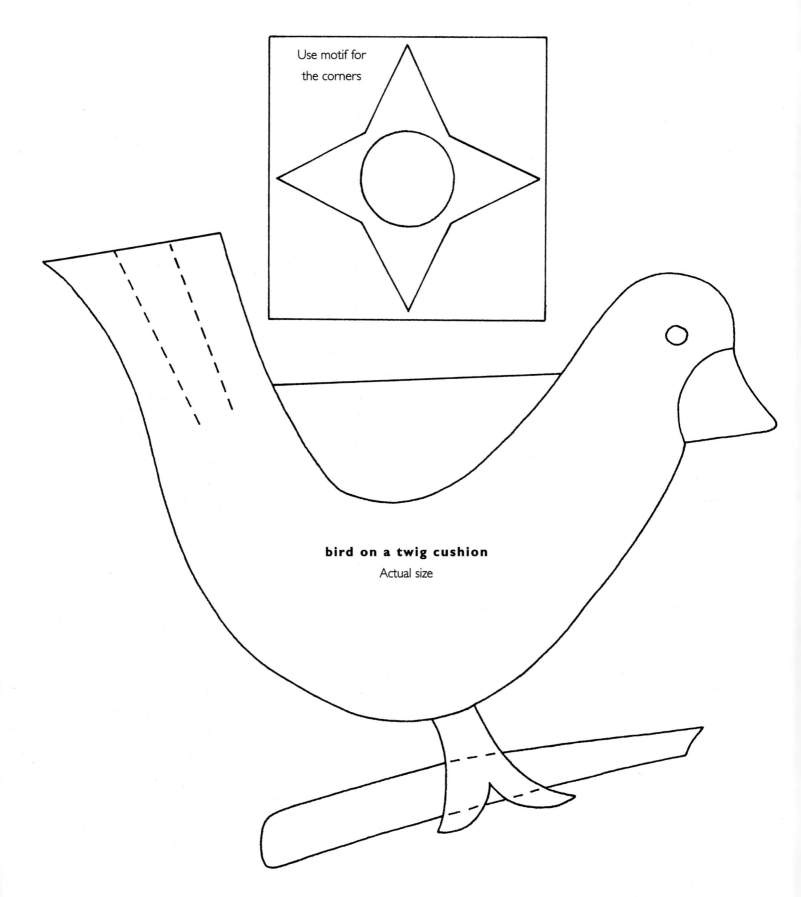

Use motif for
the corners

bird on a twig cushion
Actual size

index

acknowledgments

Many thanks to DMC for generously supplying the Cashel linen for the Painted Leaf Cushions, the Easter Tea
Cosy and all the threads; to Art Express, 12–20 Westfield Road, Leeds, West Yorkshire LS3 1DF,
Tel: 0800 731 4185, for their handmade and exotic papers used in the Autumn Lampshade and the Album
Cover: to Melin Tregwynt, Castle Morris, Haverfordwest, Pembrokeshire, Wales, UK, SA62 5UX, Tel 01348
891644, for the blanket used in the Autumn Lap Quilt; to the Natural Fabric Company for supplying the
cotton chambrays and ginghams for the Spring Table-setting and the fabric for the Garden Bench Cushion; to
Adele Corcoran for making the Bird on a Twig Cushion.

175 Seasonal Recipes